BE A BILLIONAIRE

TODAY IS THE BEST DAY TO BEGIN YOUR JOURNEY

VENKATA CHALAM RALLAPALLI

This is a humble attempt to throw light on financial planning and investment procedures which is dedicated to all the middle-class people, and the younger generation, who find it difficult to make both ends meet and who don't have any clue how to realize their financial dreams.

Nowadays, a common man doesn't understand the various investment options available to him, and blindly follows certain rich people's way of investment, without realizing that everybody is different in taking risks and understanding how it works based on various factors like risk taking ability, duration, and market conditions. Etc.

There is no authenticated or non-commercial source of information for the present younger generation, who are impatient to become wealthy. Not only are they falling prey to online frauds and attractive marketing techniques, but they are also ultimately becoming victims of unreliable sources of financial information.

On top of it, there are so many friends and relatives, who will not throw any light on the art of money management and wealth creation, but they are quick to ridicule the people who are not as prosperous as they are.

The book is an honest attempt to educatc thosc pcoplc, who wish to start their journey to become wealthy, and it is a humble and sincere attempt to give them a road map and guide them to understand the market dynamics and ultimately reach their financial goals.

I humbly dedicate this book to the growing middle class people, who are ready to take up any challenge.

$$$$$$$$$$$$

Contents

Prologue

Do you know?

Less than 3% Indian Population is directly involved in the stock market.

Remember the time you went to a multiplex with your family. You must have probably heard your grandparents say: 'Everything was so cheap back then. It's true.

Twenty years ago, the cost of movie tickets was around Rs. 40, not Rs. 500 as it is today.

Similarly, chocolates, coffee, clothes, petrol and other regular goods were much cheaper 'back then'. This phenomenon of prices rising over the years is known as inflation. It is the steady increase in the price of goods and services over time. And if you are not careful, it can eat into your savings in no time. Here's a simple example to illustrate its effect.

Imagine a chocolate bar that costs Rs. 10 today, and you have Rs. 100. With this amount, you can buy 10 chocolate bars. Over the next year, imagine you keep Rs. 100 in a bank that offers you an annual interest rate of 5%. At the end of the year, you have Rs. 105 with you.

But over one year, let's assume that the price of the chocolate bar increases to Rs. 11. This means you have to pay Rs. 110 to purchase the same 10 chocolate bars next year. But since you have only Rs. 105, you fall short of Rs. 5. This is how inflation eats into one's savings. It reduces purchasing power over time, and you have to pay more money to buy the same goods.

You can combat inflation by investing in avenues that offer you better returns over time.

While we know India as a nation of savers, millennials today tend to prefer to live in the present and enjoy the time.

Be it buying the latest gadgets, or planning an exotic holiday, the youth of today may not shy away from taking debt to fulfil such aspirations.

With the loans to service over the future, it always seems a convenient proposition.

However, servicing loan instalments, or EMIs (Equated Monthly Instalments) as they are generally referred to, calls for commitment and financial discipline, for any missed EMI may restrict access to further credit by damaging the credit score.

Making consistent SIP investments also helps you move steadily towards your financial goals and accumulate a healthy corpus over a period. So, just in case if you are planning to buy an asset, you may aim for a bigger goal with your savings. For example, if you are planning to buy a house worth Rs. 75 lakhs, you may be eligible for a home loan up to Rs. 60 lakhs. With an interest rate of 10.5% per annum and a loan tenor of 25 years, the EMI will be approx. Rs. 50,000. As such, one would have paid Rs. 1.51 crores over 25 years, including 91 lakhs interest amount.

On the other hand, you may choose to get a similar house for rent, which may be available at Rs.

15,000 to Rs. 20,000 per month, assuming a rental yield of around 2.5%. You may start a SIP EMI for the balance amount of Rs. 30,000 per month in an equity fund for 25 years and with a conservative assumption of 12% returns per annum, you may get a portfolio worth Rs. 4.20 crores by the end of the investment period. This is indeed the power of compounding, and with the fuel of 'time' propelling your financial journey, you may also aim for more significant financial goals over a long period.

As per RBI, Indian households have 95% of their wealth in physical assets, i.e., Real Estate and Gold.

Previously i.e., 20 years back, the CPI inflation used to be 2 to 3%, and even a return of Investments @5% used to beat the inflation. Now, the inflation is more than 6%, and the physical assets investments hardly get a return, which will beat the inflation.

For all present and future generations, who would like to be called as fathers, my advice is ...

Have one more digital asset child along with your natural child from the day, you are delighted to be called as "Father".

This asset child requires no schooling, no clothes, no entertainment, no pampering etc. Only regular feed.

May be, basing on financial status, every father will spend and support his child @ an average expenditure of Rs.5000/- per month.

In order to provide the comforts to the children, every father will sacrifice his comforts, neglect his health and ready to do anything.

But, after 25 years, the child whether son or daughter may not even recognize or appreciate the efforts and difficulties of their parents, in bringing up them to the present position. Even, they may blame them for not giving them enough money or assets to match their expectations. Some children may not stand on their legs, even after 25 years of support also.

Don't regret. It is your fault, if you could not get their appreciation.

The other Asset child, if you support it with Rs.5000/- per month, regularly, like another physical child, after 20 years, the child is worth more than Rs.50 lakhs. No more support. No more expectation. No more emotional blackmails.

Every year, it will give you a return gift of Rs.5 lakhs, on the "Father's Day".. every year, without break throughout your life.

It may not be the emotional support, but it is still solid support.

So, have a physical child, to have painful thrills and small celebrations and social approvals, but don't forget to have one more Asset child, who may not greet you with happy Father's Day wishes every year, but actually sends you a return gift of Rs.5 lakhs on every " Father's Day", for your support, when you are tired and desperately looking for some support.

Balance your emotional ups and downs with your rational, logical brain power. Invest in your money multiplier child. Money is every thing to sustain or nurture ... even love and affection.

Hence, those who would like to have financial independence or better aim for wealth creation, pl. remember that planning, execution and patience are the three important ingredients.

Rome was not built in a day. If you want to become a Billionaire, you have to take a firm resolution today that, I will develop the necessary skills and knowledge to become a billionaire, notwithstanding the negative circumstances.

You have to take some calculated risks and invest in opportunities, that are going to make you a billionaire over a time horizon. You have to develop the skills, to spot the opportunities, and time the market, to enter into the right investments at the right time.

Furthermore, you have to diversify your risk and diversify your investments in a such manner that it is not concentrated in any asset class or any geographical area or in one industry.

It has to be a master plan, well executed with a great precision and with a lot of patience and conviction about your ability to reach your goal.

The burning desire to become a billionaire requires patience and time. You should always look out for investment opportunities and stay abreast It with the latest business opportunities across the world. Also, ensure you develop disciplined investment habits to reach your goals soon.

Let us take a firm resolution today itself, to compound our wealth....

CHAPTER ONE

INTRODUCTION TO FINANCIAL LITERACY

Benjamin Franklin has rightly said, "If you fail to plan, you are planning to fail."

People never plan to fail ...

But very few people know about the MANAGEMENT OF money,

added to that

very few people wish to talk or discuss it because they feel that they may be treated as fools or dumb by others.

It is no exaggeration if I declare that, even though many people have a lot of qualifications and degrees, their knowledge of management of money matters or financial literacy is almost zero.

Especially in India, Financial awareness or knowledge is very low and has never been included in any of the academics as a matter of life skills, which is essential knowledge to face the challenges of life.

That's why only 2 % of the Indians participate in stock markets and only children of business families talk about investment in various alternate asset classes/ stock market, share Bazar Sensex ,etc..., right from their teenage.

How many people in the present generation know about what is the Credit Card billing cycle, what is the basis of the calculation of Interest on a loan. What is a Flat rate? What is the diminishing balancing method? Do you know the meaning of monthly compounding etc?

How many people are having the necessary knowledge and skills to choose the right investment or track its performance?

Many young educated people also do not understand the meaning of Yield, coupon rate, call /put option, etc and not to speak of derivatives, etc. How many people can understand and enjoy a financial newspaper or journals like Economic Times or Mint? Very few.

No wonder, financial literacy is not being included in the syllabus of the present education system.

Many cine artists, celebrities, and those who are in the financial sector also fail to achieve their financial freedom or live the life of their choice, only because they have not focussed on money matters or money management, in the prime of their life or career.

The present young generation commits costly mistakes in deciding financial matters because it is not discussed in the family or relatives 'circle and nobody will honestly advise them about savings, investments and multiplying the money, etc.

No college or university will teach this life skill of money management or investment strategies as a subject of general studies.

Apart from that, the discussion on money is a TABOO or " Prohibited" or restricted to only frown-

ups.

By the time they have realized or been devastated by the costly mistakes done by them, it will be too late and irreparable, as they might have developed certain behavioural patterns or belief systems from their parents or peers or society.

Hence, it has got a lot of influence or strengthened their belief system. They are also being told that,

"ALL MONEY IS BAD",

"ALL THE WEALTHY PEOPLE WILL become RICH ONLY BY ADOPTING CHEATING OR UNHOLY PRACTICES" AND

"MONEY IS THE SOURCE OF ALL EVILS"

" Money craving or aspiring to be rich make you vulnerable for lowering of moral or ethical values, and you can't become rich without compromising on ethics"

Added to this, our movies, our novels, and media always project the rich and famous in a very bad light and all our screen heroes are comparatively poor, and they will become rich only with some "LUCK".

Hence, the deeply rooted belief system, age-old rooted negative convictions on the rich people, will make you think that "you have to somehow, adjust with your means, and you have to live and adapt to the basic needs and never dream of making it big.

Living with modest means is a virtue.

Aspiring to be wealthy is inviting trouble from peers and society.

Nobody Will encourage you or motivate you to think beyond the box or tell you can realize all your financial goals, by adopting certain procedures and developing your skills.

Nobody will encourage you that you can also realize your dreams of becoming Crorepathis or multi-Millionaires by following certain tested practices and the right decisions of investments.

You need not compromise on your ethics or values, to become wealthy.

Nobody will encourage you to become a Billionaire or "filthy rich" by following the techniques of the young billionaires of the world, like other owners of Facebook or Google or Amazon.

Thanks to the present Coronavirus crisis, it has conducted the exams first to many people in their financial management and resources management, and many people have learned many harsh and bitter lessons later after the examinations are over and their results are miserably low.

That's why there is a mad rush for opening Demat accounts and searching for other alternate sources of Income.

Almost 4.9 million new demat accounts were opened during the financial year 2020, the maximum in decades, after 4 million accounts were added in the previous year.

There was a surge in retail participation in the stock market after people were forced to stay home after outbreak of the coronavirus pandemic.

Almost 35% of the present population constitutes more than 50 per cent of the active young workforce in India and they are going to be a major part of the investing public of tomorrow. This young nation does not know where to invest or what is the financial crisis until the corona has started inflicting bleeding wounds on its financial structure.

Why this new rush? Why suddenly people have been searching for alternate sources of income or so much enthusiasm towards new paths to get money and reach their financial goals.

Why should I acquire or improve my Financial awareness or literacy?

Spiralling Inflation:

Old people always remark: 'Everything was so cheap in our days".

It's true. Twenty-five years ago, the cost of movie tickets was around Rs. 10 and not Rs. 200.

The cost of a cup of Tea is Rs.1, not Rs 10/-

We have constructed an independent house at a cost of Rs.3 lakhs in the year 1980,

Now, you cannot even imagine a small room with that kind of budget.

Hence, inflation is eating away all our hard-earned money and many people find it difficult to make both ends meet.

The present Corona pandemic and our total dependence on crude oil imports have escalated the Cost of living like never before, and it is going to impact our cost of living in every sphere.

About 40 years back, 4a -figure salary was considered to be the envy of all others. Getting a four-figure salary of Rs.1000/ p.m is considered to be the ultimate dream of an average salary earner.

Now, even a seven-figure salary also appears to be not very satisfactory, due to the change in lifestyle, global exposure and changing expectations of the present generation.

Inflation reduces purchasing power over a period of time and you have to pay increasingly more and more fo the same product service. It erodes your money value and over a period of time, it starts giving negative returns on your conventional type of investments.

"Money will not be grown on trees". Hence, we have to be careful while spending and saving.

Your degrees and knowledge may not automatically result in wealth or cthe umulation of assets. College Degrees or your skill only make you eligible for some job r profession, but nodo make you rich overnight. You will end up living from pay cheque to pay cheque or hand to mouth existence.

As per the press reports..." Nearly two-thirds of Americans, 63%, say they've been living pay cheque to pay cheque since the Covid-19 pandemic hit the U.S. earlier this year".

About 42% of Americans report taking on more debt than they normally would, and over a quarter of survey respondents say they've accumulated more than $10,000 in new debt since the pandemic started.

It is no different in India.

More than 60% of people have been informed that they are spending more than their income and more than ⅔ of Indian Youth don't know how to survive and live, if they are sacked from their present employment, due to pandemic-related economic job losses.

It is not the desire of becoming wealthy, it is the struggle for existence, struggle for basic needs of life, it is the widening gap between their expenditure and income, that has made the people tome out of their deep-rooted financial habits, and now they are forced to go for new financial habits, or they may face the harsh realities of life and perish.

But if you want to become a crorepati or multi-billionaire, you need to possess the specialized knowledge and mmindset to plan and execute the financial plans into reality with perseverance, determination and grit.

Like a family doctor for health, you need the advice of a financial advisor to realize your dreams or have a clear road map for your comfortable financial life journey.

2. Lifestyle traps:

UNLIMITED DESIRES AND LIMITED INCOME:

Similarly... the present youth ....Lifestyle traps....

The present generation are gadget freaks.

They love partying, they love social media, they want to have lunch or dinners at the most expensive hotels and every other person wants to travel to the best tourist locations and travelling is one of the attractive hobbies.

The fancy dresses, the dazzling bikes and ever alluring cars and gadgets make the people more and more consumerist and craving for more and bigger.

Their desires are endless, and their budget is limited.

3.Personal loans and credit card culture:

Apart from the above, easy availability of credit card culture. Previously, people used to earn and then spend.

Nowadays, thanks to the easy availability of credit cards, personal loans etc, people are borrowing at very high rates and spending lavishly.

But many people do not understand how much they are repaying by their EMIs. By the time they are about to close one loan, they will be tempted to take one more Credit Card Advance or Bill, which will put them eternally in the debt trap.

Many people think that it is too early to start thinking about saving or planning for some investments as their income is perceived to be very limited, and they are finding it difficult to cope up with their lifestyle needs.

They always postpone things, waiting for some good amount to be received to go for any type of major investments.

4.Growth of SENIOR CITIZENS and Average life expectancy:

Thanks to the increased health care and better medical facilities, average life expectancy has increased from 27 in the year 1947 to 72 after 70 years of independence.

What does it mean? More non-earning life than the earning life. More expenditure after retirement

than ability to generate income or salary.

BY 2031 India WILL HAVE 17.9 CRORES senior citizen population and by the year 2041 India will have 24 CR Senior citizen population. More than 85% of people don't have any permanent, assured or reliable source of Income.

Apart from the lack of assured source of Income, Most of the Indians, does not have ANY KNOWLEDGE ABOUT

Majority Senior Citizens prefer FD's and Post Office Investments.

Interest rates on these both products are becoming less and less day by day.

Do you know?

Less than 1.5 % of Indian Population Invests in Mutual Fund, i.e Out of 134 Crores only 2 Crores Mutual Fund Investors are there. Thus, there is a HUGE SCOPE in this sector

Mutual Funds - One of the Fastest growing products in Financial Investment Sector

Mutual Funds Assets Under Management has grown 3 times in last 5 years with 25% Annual Growth

A Unique Investment Instrument which takes care of your short term needs and Long term goals

5. No GOVT JOBS OR NO GUARANTEE OF ASSURED JOB OR PROFESSION:

Now the trend is Public Sector to Private Sector in India. Most of the jobs are being outsourced or privatised and GiG economy or totally need based jobs are being created.

What is the impact? No more security of Job or Assured Income. You are not sure how many years you will last in the present job or profession or trade. Hence, everybody is searching for other streams of Income or passive income resources.

6. Nuclear families and no dependence on children:

Thanks to the availability of advanced techniques and procedures of medicines, the average life expectancy of the average human being has increased from 27 years to 72 years, since independence. Hence, your chances of spending more inactive years than the active years may result in erosion of your lifetime savings within a short period, if you are not productive or if have no other sources of Income, apart from your savings.

You may not get the support of joint family or children's support due to increased stress on human relations and proliferation of nuclear families.

7. Globalization and impact of Global resources:

Thanks to rapid Globalization, and adapting to the universal economic and investment policies, the interest rates on traditional Savings and Household income is dwindling year-on-year, in tandem with the interest rates prevailing in the Developed countries like USA, Japan and some European countries. The traditional investments methods of Bank FDs, Gold and Real Estate may not beat the inflation and there is an urgent need to fall in line with the global practices of channelizing the household savings to more financial assets or paper-based products.

8. Awakening of young millennials to the harsh realities of life:

The present young generation is prepared to upskill or unlearn in order to participate in the new economic revolution or knowledge revolution that is happening through smart smartphones, Adhar enabled onboarding boarding, faster connectivity and growing support of technology. Now the younger generation is learning the tricks of the trade faster so that they want to participate in the companies, either manufacturing or service oriented companies, in order to participate in their growth momentum.

There is a lot of economic awareness created by the harsh realities of life and constant threat to the continuity of their jobs or profession and the present educated global millennials are prepared to take the extra mile to improve their financial independence to support their lifestyle and ambitions.

9. India is poor country as per Human Development Index:

India is still a poor country.. As far as the Human Development Index is concerned ... hence 80% of people are still struggling to meet their basic needs and still have no clue how to realize their financial goals.

10. Availability of more technical tools and opening of the power of technology for fast operations and with minimum effort:

Thanks to the Adhar and 4g /5 g connectivity and affordable internet connectivity, more and more people can now join the new avenues of investment like stock markets, commodities markets etc... without much trouble and with the help of several apps.

****

CHAPTER TWO

STEPS IN FIXING FINANCIAL GOALS

"We always overestimate the change that will occur in the next two years and underestimate the change that will occur in the next ten. Don't let yourself be lulled into inaction." – Bill Gates

Many people do not have any plan for their future. They simply go by the tide/ or present situation.

They live for today only. Likewise, they will get carried away by their impulsive actions or their unplanned expenses, which are totally triggered by their moods or impulses.

They somehow adjust or just exist, but not have any concrete ideas about their future. They seem to be not perturbed by the lack of any planning or any solid road map for future events, whether planned or not.

Over a period of time, it becomes their basic nature, and they brag about their unpreparedness for the future as a virtue. They tend to project their lack of planning as a sign of their strength and intelligence.

They believe in the idea of " somehow we will manage" and always do the fire fighting. The "Karma" or " Naseeb" theory or Philosophical quotes will be used as a support for their plain laziness or inaction. These people are not action oriented. They are only deliver sermons.

Each of us has dreams, buying a car or a house, a grand marriage, happy retirement, etc.

Each of these life goals has a monetary impact attached to it, along with the obvious emotional angle and sacrifice angle.

But life is not always the same. We have our ups and downs and life exams will begin without any announcement, and all of a sudden.

Whether you have an emergency fund or not, whether you have the financial capacity or not, the emergency event or time will not stop, and it has no mercy or grace period to face it. Whether it is a medical emergency of our near or dear or Unexpected loss or theft or any other loss or risk, it will come without giving any forewarning or clue.

At that time only, many people will learn their first lesson about the need for money and management of it and saving for a rainy day. They understand by then, with a bitter taste, that money is the most important thing to overcome any difficulty or trouble, and not providing for it or even anticipating it is a big mistake.

Many people do not understand the value of time and the principle of compounding.

Many people do not comprehend the value of the future value of money and its impact on our decisions.

A. For example, **Rajesh** Started investing at the age of 25 with a SIP amount of Rs,10,000/- Per Month up to the age of 60 i.e., total period of 35 years.

His total investment is(Rs.10,000*35*12) Rs.42 lakhs, and it may grow to a sum of Rs.5.51 crores by the age of 60. Assuming an annualized return of 12% PA.

A. While **Suresh** started investing at the age of 35 with a SIP of Rs,25,000 up to the age of 60, i.e. for a period of 25 years.

Whereas the total investment Rs.75 lakhs of Mr. Suresh may grow

to Rs. 4,27 crores only- @ an annualized expected average return of 12%.

Why this difference? The compounding wonder of time. It is the eight wonders of the world.

Longer you stay invested, the more you will get in the compound rate.

Hence, start investing as early as possible, once you start earning or

today only when you have decided to become rich.

STEPS IN FIXING FINANCIAL GOALS:

a. **HAVE A WRITTEN FINANCIAL GOAL:**

"Someone's sitting in the shade today because someone planted a tree a long time ago"

Warren Buffett

We have to begin somewhere. It is not too LATE to begin.

- It is high time that we have to take a concrete step to start.
- Ultimately, the action only makes you rich .....not thinking.
- Unless you have belief in yourself, you can not start.
- So, have clear-cut goals and financial objectives, **preferably written ones, which are pasted and seen every day.**

B. WHAT IS A FINANCIAL GOAL?

All human beings will have dreams and desires. But many of them will remain as dreams only because they are not achievable, but we have not done enough homework to make them achievable by giving ***a hazy idea to the subconscious mind.***

Let me explain in simple terms..

Everybody's wish is to have a dream house. But we will not go deep into it, and we are not specific about this dream. We simply think of owning a house. But the subconscious does not have a granularity or clarity, what does it really mean? Is it a thatched house or a luxurious mansion? When it has to be acquired? during the next month or at old age? How much is the cost of a house? Is it just Rs. one lakh or One billion?

Hence, in order to realize any financial goal, it has got two important or salient features

What is a financial Goal ......1. It should always be expressed in monetary terms.

2. It should always have a time frame and deadline.

Hence, the financial goal of " I want to have a house " *should be reframed as*

I would like to a have a 2-bedroom flat at Hyderabad @ Rs.60 lakhs

Within a period of 5 years time i.e. before May 2026,.

If available, you can have **a model house photo** affixed on the sheet and

You can have a much more granularity, on the proposed house....., ie

how many sq. ft,

- other Facilities,
- area preference,
- whether under construction or ready to move flat,
- whether within the city or in suburbs,
- what is the loan amount, what is the initial down payment etc.

You should write it down, or get it printed and paste it in a conspicuous place, where you can see it every day.

Your action point #1: Immediately write down your most important financial goal on a paper incorporating the above two salient features and with all the details and preferably a photo.

After preparation pl. Paste it at a place where it can be seen by you every day. Even others may laugh at or ridicule it ... don't pay any attention.

B. GAP ANALYSIS: WHAT IS YOUR PRESENT FINANCIAL STATUS OR RESOURCES TO REACH THE GOAL AGAINST THE ESTIMATED COST.

Any financial goal requires massive follow-up action and detailed plan of execution in order to start your journey to reach the goal.

For this important step, we have to take stock of our present resources and our financial capacity or possible sources of income to implement it. It is nothing but a conscious and honest assessment of our available resources to implement it immediately and with an objective to project the gap between the cost of the Project and the present state of our financial resources.

If we have a clear idea about, what is the estimated cost of our financial dream and what is the present status of our financial state, then we can precisely arrive at the gap analysis, with time frame and milestones.

Initially, it may appear to be overwhelming or daunting and beyond our capacity. We may feel initially discouraged or lose our initial enthusiasm to reach this financial goal.

But no challenge is a challenge, unless it should appear as difficult & formidable at the first glance.

Never set any financial goal, which is easily achievable and which is very much affordable with your present financial position.

Because it is not making you any richer or wealthier, and you are not getting any benefit out of this mediocre attitude or average, ordinary person's mind set.

No financial goal is worth trying, unless it initially appears to be impossible and beyond your present capacity.

But., the moment you have made up your mind and resolved yourself to reach the goal, all the forces in the world will somehow conspire to support you and to ensure the ultimate success of your financial dream.

But, first you have to overcome the initial hesitancy, initial doubts, initial fear of failure and once you firmly resolve to pursue it, new vistas will open up, and you will realize that you are tapping into new power centers and new financial avenues to make enough money to achieve them.

Once you decide, never turn back.

C: MASSIVE ACTION AND DETAILED PLAN OF EXECUTION:

1. **Step no. 1:Start writing down.**

All your financial goals or dreams, irrespective of whether they are needs or desires or absolute nonsense.

Eg. to give some examples of financial goals.

1. construct/ buy a house or residential land
2. Modify or renovate the house
3. Buy a four-wheeler/ SUV
4. Upgrade the present car/ bike
5. SON/DAUGHTER higher education.
6. son/daughter .. ABROAD studies
7. son/ daughter marriage/ settlement
8. Foreign tour/ destination wedding
9. Purchase of 2nd house
10. Retirement fund
11. Diamond jewellery or Gold
12. Farmhouse
13. New business or venture
14. Migration to a foreign country by investment.

Step no. 2. Prioritize them... a.as per absolute necessary/need

a.needs: eg: Vehicle for commuting to office or colleges.

House for residence etc

Child education.

May be needed as per the individual choice and social standing.

b. Comfort: upgrading to more expensive cars/vehicles

c. Luxury: diamond necklace/ foreign trips

d. Aspirational: Farmhouse/ settlement abroad

Step No: 3 : fill the expected cost of the financial goal with details and time horizon and deadlines.

Eg: for purchase of a House: cost components:

1. Cost of land
2. Cost of stamps and registration.
3. Construction cost
4. Cost of amenities like parking, generator, security etc.
5. Cost of assessment and other legal formalities
6. Cost of addl. Facilities and like false ceilings/ modular kitchen,grills, decorative paintings, lights, sanitary accessories etc.
7. Cost of taxes, insurance and other maintenance.
8. Any other related cost, which is part of the project.

Step N0.4: Detailed cost of each component and your present financial capacity to meet the expenditure and time frame and deadline to meet the expenditure.

Step no. 5: Prioritize and sort.

Before finalizing your financial goals, first of all, you have to prioritize and give preference to your absolute and basic needs, followed by your good-to-have needs or desires and lastly your luxuries.

Step no. 6: Gap Analysis

Once you have rearranged the financial goals, as per their rationality and urgency, you have to arrive at the GAP ANALYSIS, which is the difference between the estimated cost of your goal and the present availability of funds or resources.

Step No. 7: Sorting as per Tenor

ARRANGE THE FINANCIAL GOALS IN THE ORDER OF SHORT TERM, MEDIUM-TERM AND LONG TERM. Because different time duration requires, different tools and different plants to reach them. Time and Risk bearing capacity will decide the schemes or plans to achienve them.

Step no. 8: the present resources

what are the available sources of income as of today or in the near future to meet the respective goals should be entered in an excel sheet or on a Table.

Step no. 9. Enter the estimated cost of each goal

How much is the estimated cost of the goal, taking into account inflation cost and other allied expenses after the estimated time period and taking into account the future cost of that goal. It is very crucial to arrive at the gap analysis and to estimate the time and effort required to reach the goal.

Step no. 10. what is the gap between present resources and estimated cost of the goal

Arrive at the Gap between the cost of the goal and the availability of present sources of funds. The more accurate the estimate and calculation, the better the possibility of arriving at the estimated time and cost and accordingly successful plan of action to reach the goal.

Model FINANCIAL GOALS/ DETAILS/ MODEL TABLE :

a. Name of the goal , Prioritise (need/desire/ luxury/ others),

b.Estimated time frame and deadline

c,date/month/year

d,Short term/ medium term/Long term

e.The estimated cost of the goal Rs,

f.Present sources of funds Rs.

g.Gap amount Rs.

h. Plan of action to fill the gap and time required.

Example:

House purchase, need,6 years.. 6 years from today.

5 yrs, Medium Term., 60 L estimated cost , 5 Lakhs ... present resources.

Rs,55 Lakhs ... gap amount to reach the goal.

5 years; estimated time ; estimated gap amount Rs. 10 lakhs per annum. total Rs. 55 lakhs.

<u>**Please arrange all your needs/ necessaties/ good to have items/ dreams/ in the order**</u>

of duration ie immediate/shortterm/medium Term/ Long Term etc. with their estimated cost

eg.

1.Motor bike 2. Car 3.House 4.Children Education 5. Foreign Tour 6. Villa 7. Diamond necklace

along with estimated cost of each of the above, with duration etc.

It is very important to write it down on a paper, as per time lines, so that necessary Financial planning can be done, and necessary schemes may be planned to meet the objectives as per time line.

Step No. 11: ARRANGE THEM IN THE ORDER OF TIME FRAME

ie Immediate need/ short need/ Medium Term need/ Long term need.

Step No.12: Planning for the important stages of life events:

From the date of your earning money or employment or profession to the date of your proposed date of retirement. Pl. list all the life stage events and financial goals spanning a period of 30 to 35 years upto the date of retirement. What are the major events and your preparedness for the major milestones of your life. What is your preparedness for children's education, your preparedness for sudden illness or sickness of beloved and your planning for loss of job or health.

Step 13: plan for emergency fund :

Planning for emergencies is always necessary, whether you like it or not. It is like a reserve in a Vehicle. Accident is one which can not be predicted or planned. Hence, in life, anything may happen. For those unknown and unprepared events the fund will come to our rescue. It should be a minimum 6 times of your average last six months monthly expenditure. Suppose your average monthly expenditure for the last 6 months is Rs.50,000/- , you should maintain an emergency fund of 50*6=Rs.3,00,000/- always, which can be used with a short notice.

Step 14: plan for protection from unexpected loss of life, health, job,income and reputation etc.

As per the Maslow's hierarchy of needs..

the needs are: physiological (food and clothing), safety (job security), love and belonging needs (friendship), esteem, and self-actualization.

Hence, after Physiological needs, we have to plan for Safety needs, love and belonging needs and then esteem needs.

Hence adequate planning should be done to evaluate the risk of unpredicted risk of loss of life, health, earning capacity, loss of property etc. to safeguard ourselves from unknown perils or risks.

Step 15: plan for retirement :

This is the most important aspect of planning, which is more relevant in India. In India, 85% of people do not have any assured income after their retirement and the majority of people does not have any idea how much it will cost in future to continue the same lifestyle.

Whenever we are estimating the cost of any event or item, we have to account for the cost of inflation and accordingly the future value of that event should be arrived at.

The probable return on investments(ROI) should be taken on a conservative basis and going by the historical data.

Step 16:Estate planning and succession planning:

This step is always neglected by the Financial planners and those who are aware of the importance also, because of some misconceptions and age-old perceptions.

It is a last but not the least important step, to protect our wealth and ensure that the property and wealth is passed on to the persons, after the departure of life, as per the person's wish or will. There is no scope for legal action or interpretation.

The estate planning objective is to pass on the wealth or income to their beloved ones without any hassles and without following any tedious legal procedures, in the unfortunate event of their sudden exit from this world.

MODEL CHART OF LIFE STAGES/ MAJOR EVENTS AND FINANCIAL PLANNING

Life stage / Major event /Financial action /Remarks

a.First stage

Adulthood/student

Education plan/livelihood plan. Search for better options and settlement. Skill enhancement and professional/business plans.

No Income or dependent on scholarships/. Loans and funding sources. etc

b.Second stage

Joining in a job or profession

Purchase of essentials ..e.g..

vehicles/ furniture/house plots. Ability to take risk and rewarding options.

Income is limited and requires more efforts for passive income

c.Third stage

Marriage

Protection and Insurance plans. Expand the plan to include the spouse and children. Develop the financial planning & thrift plans. High yield investment portfolio

Planning for enhancing the income and other sources of income/ High yield investment knowledge and risk taking ability.

d.Fourth stage

Middle age with children

Financial goals and alignment of investments as per the time plan.

Plan for higher education/protection needs.Moderate risk appetite.

e.Fifth stage

Before Retirement

Portfolio rebalancing and allotment of assets as per risk tolerance.

Withdrawal of savings and investments for the discharge of major family responsibilities.

Major rebalancing of assets and future planning.

Prepare for the unforeseen events or losses.

f.Sixth stage

After retirement

Planning for assured Monthly income; Annuities,Monthly Income Plans.

Health insurance;

Reduction of risk based assets;

Estate planning

Ability to earn may be reduced. The responsibilities and commitments may be continued and added. burden.

WHY SHOULD WE PLAN FOR LIFE EVENTS: is it worth ? can we travel with flow?

If you are failing to plan, you are planning to fail or you may never be ready for tomorrw.

Planning removes the pain or suffering of not doing the homework properly and not preparing ourselves for life events and realities of life.

Some lessons or takeaways from our favourite C(crazy)topics:

India is always mad about 3 Cs. 1. Cinema 2.Cricket 3. Controversial topics.

From Cricket, we can learn some lessons :

a.Too much defensive may not always be the right path to win the match.

Especially during the IPL, defence is not a virtue.

When you have limited time and expected scoring rate is very high, no defence will work.

It does not mean that we have to be very aggressive and end up in duck out.

There is a midway between defence and offence and take calculated risk and increase the run rate.

Similarly in Investment also, we have to take a midway between conservative and aggressive ness.

b. Opportunities and time wait for none:

The time and overs will not wait for none, whether you make use of it or not.

The ship is built for withstanding the storms and cyclones also, if necessary. It is not meant to be anchored at the shore.

For the prepared and well educated investor, every seemingly risk may turn out to be an opportunity to make a fortune, with his calculated risk taking ability and converting the challenges to the advantages. Action is important for winning.

Hence, wehter you are prepared or not, the life stages will come and responsibilities will increase automatically, as per the time frame, once you are married and you are becoming older day by day. It is better to be prepared than feel sorry.

Sometimes, it is a futile and uphill task, to repent on the lost opportunity and wasted time.

Do take action and do it consistently towards a better tomorrow and plan for a rainy day.

c.Unity in diversity is the strength.

The team consists of different players with different capabilities and weakness.

The team as a whole matters, not the individual strengths or weaknesses. How best you are as a team,

is the most important point for success.

With a focus on making a healthy return, the investment portfolio should have a healthy mix of diversified capital funds and diversified industries and diversified products. Ultimately, in the event of any economic ups and downs, ***the diversity will protect us from total collapse and works as a shock absorber.***

To conclude.... A journey of a thousand miles starts from the first step...

At the cost of repetition....

- **We have to begin somewhere. It is not too early or too late to begin.**
- **It is high time that we have to take a concrete step to start.**
- **Unless you have belief in yourself, you can not start.**

- **So, have clear cut goals and financial objectives, preferably written ones, which are pasted and seen every day.**

Pl. write it down on a piece of paper and paste it in a conspicuous place.

“Let me put it bluntly: anyone who says money isn’t important doesn’t have any!”

if you think money is not important it will never come to you”

If you think you are rich or you are poor--- you are absolutely right.....

As per the Bhagvadgita, You can decide what you want to be.

“*Your thoughts will manifest into deeds, and deeds will transform into results.*”

****

CHAPTER THREE

WHAT ARE THE COMMON MYTHS AND PROBLEMS

"If you want to move to a higher level of life, you have to be willing to let go of some of your old ways of thinking and being and adopt new ones".

Some common Myths and roadblocks to implementing the action program:

1. ***"All the statements you heard about money when you were young remain in your subconscious mind as part of the blueprint that is running your financial life".***

But the best part is your subconscious mind can be reprogrammed and you can start a new set of instructions to your mind at any time, if you are passionate about it.

1. ***"Financial planning is easier said than done"***

True. But for that matter, any change or any discipline is not easy in the beginning.

What is hard in the beginning will give you lasting benefits in the long run.

3. ***"I don't have any permanent job or my source of income is not assured. How can I start implementing it?"***

It is like waiting for the waves to recede at the beach to enter into the sea for a swim.

Enjoy surfing and develop the ability or skill to raid the waves of uncertainty, instead of eternally waiting for the ideal time.

4. ***"I am too young to think of my retirement or saving for a rainy day. Let me enjoy the sunshine of my prime life with parties, friends, and vacations before it is too late".***

You will realize the cost of delay only in the evening of life, when it is too late.

The friends will accompany you as long as you have money and wealth. Along with the money, your friends and parties will also suddenly disappear, once your income sources are dried up and once your overspending makes you penniless.

5. ***"I am too young to think of my retirement corpus, and I am quite healthy to think of my health or life insurance"***

Retirement means, not old age or after 60 years of age, it is the age where you need not depend upon any source of income for the execution of your financial goals.

It can be earlier than you think. It can be middle age or any time, when you have the financial independence to carry out your ideas or plan of action, at your absolute choice and as per your passion and interest. You need to change your mind because you have no funds or resources to support it.

6. ***"My present occupation or job is very rewarding, and I am highly skilled. I need not take care of my future as I am the most sought-after person in the field."***

Nobody is permanent, and No skill is going to last forever. Anything may happen at any time, and it doesn't take much time to become bankrupt or become most useful to a useless product or person.

Rapid technological changes, new innovations, and ever-changing habits may totally change the scenario and new disruptions and thoughts may cause 360-degree changes.

Hence, be prepared for the fast-moving changes and ever-changing new innovations and technologies.

7. ***"I have inherited a lot of wealth and property. My property will last for the next two generations".***

People have no idea how the Ice of wealth will simply melt away, if you are not proactive in protecting it.

You can't imagine how one misadventure may result in total scene reversal. Ask any cine Producer or some celebrities about their change of fortunes and their riches to rags stories.

8. ***"My hand to mouth existence will not give any chance for any savings. How can I aspire to be a wealthy person?"***

If any limitation is there,it exists in one's thinking, it is in their mind and their thinking. Once you have made a firm commitment to become wealthy, new and innovative thoughts and doors will open up before you to reach the goal.

You are going to find new empowerment in you which is not yet tapped or explored so far.

Only thing is, you should be ready to explore and tap the new ways of prosperity and willing to pay the price for it with utmost faith and trust in your capability to reach the goal.

Behavioural Biases in Investment Decision-Making

A. Irrational behaviour and emotionally driven decisions:

Many people do not understand the dynamics of Investment patterns and ecosystems. They always try to compare the return with their limited knowledge of fixed assets and expect the same pattern or return within a shorter period.

They tend to expect the fruits, even before the roots are deeply planted and even without nurturing the money trees.

People have very little patience and perseverance. Their greed for immediate return or astronomical returns is legendary.

B. Excessive greed and excessive fear

These are the two important factors which are the root cause for the financial crimes and white collar criminals to loot the gullible public.

These unscrupulous cheaters will attract the investors with attractive returns and promise them 3 or 4 times of normal returns to trap them in fraudulent schemes. Their excessive greed is the main reason for their ultimate loss of their total investment within a shorter period.

Similarly, excessive fear is resulting in erosion of wealth and ultimate reduction in the real value of money over a period of 10 to 20 years.

Most people rely on examples or experiences that come to mind immediately while analysing any investment plans or options to invest.

C: No research or knowledge about available options:

This leads to missing out on critical information, especially pertaining to various investment risks. People do not have enough data or research papers to make a decision on various available options, and they simply follow the herd mentality.

It means that they are not aware of the Pros and cons of their choice and tend to follow the crowd.

D. Familiarity Bias:

Change is always viewed with suspicion. Novelty is daunting and sometimes does not contribute to peace of mind. Hence, we take comfort in following the familiar route to avoid the initial discomfort and missing the total advantages of new options.

E. Herd Mentality :

"Man is a social animal" –

While this behaviour has helped our ancestors to gain upper hand in the jungle, this often works against investors' interests in financial decisions.

F: Loss Aversion:

Loss aversion means.. Investors prefer to avoid losses or taking risks in order to take better gains or returns. Such behaviour often leads people to stay away from profitable opportunities, due to the perception of high risks, however small risk it may be.

G : Overconfidence :

Over a period of time, some people blindly believe in their ability to make profits in the market and in this mental condition of overconfidence in their ability, sometimes they make decisions without weighing the other available better options, leading to financial loss and grief.

****

CHAPTER FOUR

VARIOUS STEPS IN FINANCIAL PLANNING

"Financial planning is the process which provides you a framework for achieving your life goals in a systematic and planned way by avoiding shocks and surprises"- unknown

Manage your Money/Income/ salary...

1.Prepare a personal budget.

How many of you are maintaining a small notebook, noting down all your monthly expenses and how your salary is being spent in a month?

How many of you are having a detailed excel sheet or a simple table, tracking your every payment and grouping them in the appropriate expenses head?

Sounds weird? Too fussy? Old-fashioned? Yes.

Some younger generation are very fast and furious in spending.

They wait for 28 days to get the salary credited, and it hardly takes two days to spend all that salary. Sound familiar?

Money Management will be much easier if you have a good tracking system and if you have a clear-cut idea how you are spending money and what are your expenditure heads. You can do an analysis of your monthly expenditure or quarterly expenditure to have a better knowledge of which type of expenditure is the major one and where there is no control over expenditure.

IF you don't have the habit of noting down your expenditure, pl. Start doing it immediately. Purchase a small pocket notebook or better download an app on your mobile for personal budget and start entering each and every rupee that you are spending.

Set a monthly budget and enter the actual amount of expenditure to review it later.

Like a bank cashier, Pl. have a perfect receipts and payments notebook with you and if possible carry it with you. Always try to have both a physical and digital notebook with you to monitor and analyse the present cash outflow and inflow.

Once you maintain it for at least 3 months in a sequence, you will understand your spending pattern, where the money is flowing and how the money is being spent on various heads. Once you are convinced that more money is being spent on avoidable expenditure, your first step towards Financial planning is already taken.

PERSONAL BUDGET FOR THE MONTH OF ____________2021.

EXPENDITURE TYPE

PRESENT AMT.Rs.

PROJECTED/Budget Rs

DIFFERENCE

REMARKS

A. **Fixed expenditure:**

A:Essential Groceries and food items:

Cereals, pulses, oils, bakery, sugar, Tea/coffee/beverages, vegetables, fruits, eggs, meat, fish, etc.

B: Housing... rent, maintenance, Elty, taxes etc.

C. Transportation: Petrol, repairs, maintenance, servicing etc. Metro pass etc

D: COMMUNICATION/CONNECTIVITY: Phone bills, net/ MOBILE /INTERNET CHARES ETC

E: HEALTH CARE: Medicines, Tonics, Dr fees/ supplements etc

F: Education: school fees, Books, Transportation, tuition fees etc

G: children care : Medicines, checkup, dresses, Toys etc

H: others: servant / newspaper/ EMI /mortgage exp. etc

B: variable Expenditure:

a. **Outside dining/ entertainment**

a. **Recreation, parties, movies etc**

c. **Functions, gifts, Festivals**

D: emergency / adhoc expd.

E: others

Total expenditure (A+B)

surplus/ Deficit

TOTAL NET INCOME OR SALARY

Total surplus for present/ financial goals

2. Regulate your VARIABLE EXPENDITURE :

Once you maintain your financial diary without any break, you can find out the loop holes and the expenditure types, which are draining your money and

You can easily identify that expenditure head, which is the main contributing factor for your surplus income or deficit income.

Most of us will spend, to maintain a High profile or to project an inflated image,

Many people live on perpetual fake prestige or projected social image, by wasting so much of money and their efforts.

Most of the social functions and amount spent on fancy gadgets, fancy cars and appearances are some expenses, which are not at all good for ultimate financial health and if you are now regularly spending on unnecessary items, the time will come when you have to sell your essential properties

Buying an expensive car or spending all your savings on a big house or lavish expenditure on the Birthday or engagement parties are some wasteful expenditures, which can be avoided for a temporary or fleeting pleasure, which is not real.

Please realize that real recognition and real value enhancement comes automatically once you are financially independent and become wealthy. It is a long term game and permanent.

It doesn't mean that you have to live a life without any celebrations or enjoy life's little memorable days. Regulation is the mantra and avoidance.

Never imitate anybody just for the sake of false prestige or instant gratification. Be yourself and spend your amount after earning it and once you are convinced that you deserve it.

3. Prepare a detailed Financial plan in the descending order of urgency and importance, as discussed earlier.

<u>Urgent and Immediate financial needs:</u>

Assess your present financial position and find out whether the estimated amount of a personal financial goal can be reached with the present income or surplus, taking into account the time available and estimated amount saved or earmarked on that date of the goal.

To illustrate, as a young father, you would like to join your child in a prestigious KG school with a budget of Rs. Two lakhs initially and recurring expenditure of Rs.25,000/- every month after two years from now.

You have to project the present savings for the next two years and calculate whether your present financial status and earnings will meet the demand on that projected date.

You have to design a specific plan and allocation of funds for reaching your immediate and urgent needs, without any ambiguity or without any if and buts.

The urgent and immediate needs can not be postponed or avoided at the 11th hour and sometimes, we have to pay heavy price for not providing for this type of immediate expenditure.

Hence, enough precautions have to be taken to see that the plan is foolproof and the estimated amount should be available for meeting the need, under any circumstances.

Once you achieve the immediate and urgent financial goals without much pain, naturally your morale will be high, and you will get a confidence that your planning and journey on the road to realizing your financial dreams is working,

The small successes and achievements have to be celebrated and diarized, so that neural pathways in your brain will be increased, and you are motivated to attempt for a better and bigger dreams realization, following the same baby steps.

4. Plan for Mid term goals i.e. more than year -- up to 5 years

Many young people have expressed doubts that, "what is the use of Budgeting and planning when they do not have any income at present" Yes. You can always improve your position, at least from today.

If you were born poor, it is not your mistake. If you are going to die poor, it is your mistake only.

How many people are ready to put in extra effort or upskill, in order to develop their chances of realizing their dreams.

How many are really understand the concept of money multiplying or making money.

How many of you are encouraged to seek a passive income, at an early age by your elders or friends.

How many are interested in learning the basics of becoming rich?

But the difference between success and failure lies in your belief system. Your conviction.

A poor person always say " I can't afford it"

Whereas a Rich person will always think "How am I going to afford it".

Once you are committed to the goal and exploring the ways and means to get the money, automatically your thinking and vibrations of your thoughts will somehow make it happen.

It is not a blind prophecy. It has happened several times with repeated regularity.

Once, when I was delivering my lecture on the same subject at a college, one young student has interrupted me and with the question

" How do you expect me to dream of a bike of Rs.one lakh sir, when I have no money even to pay for my college fees?"

Then I retorted and asked, "How strong is your desire to have a bike? "

He said, "I am ready to do anything sir to get my dream bike sir"

Then I asked him, what is your speciality? In which activity or field are you interested?

For this, he answered rather casually with a mischievous smile, "I am interested in chit-chatting with friends and roaming around the city with them".

Then I countered him, "I am ready to recommend you to a permanent job in a reputed MNC, which involves roaming around the city and talking with a lot of people ,,,, after some silence... I continued...

" But you have to execute a Service Bond for one year ... are you ready?"

"Are you ready for the opportunity?" I repeated the offer again...

Then he started thinking and could not say yes or no immediately. His face became red and he could not look at me and became nervous.

Then I continued.. To assure him....

"If you are going to take up the job and do it continuously for two months with all sincerity, you are going to get your bike in the third month itself, and you will be the owner of the bike after one year".

There was total silence in the hall and the situation became a bit serious and tense.

The student, who had started with the intention to hijack my lecture and wanted to get the limelight of the other students could not continue further and without saying anything, he preferred to slip into an introspective mood.

This was a real life incident and The offer of Job was also genuine and real.

Many people have many dreams, but they are not yet ready to take necessary action to achieve it, or they have no idea how to realize their dreams.

Any person, who is passionate about his / her dreams will grab the offer and is ready to sacrifice their time, effort and talent to realize the dreams.

In India, thanks to the British rule, all Indians have forgotten about "Entrepreneurship", self development and Personal growth. Our outdated education system is preparing us for " entry level jobs, marketing jobs or routine jobs, with no personal growth or scope for wealth creation or self-reliance.

There is no support for " vocational training " of skill development, to become self-reliant and provide employment to others instead of looking for employment.

Those who think that their present income is not sufficient to meet the goal, immediately expand their horizon and start thinking of improving their skills or looking for sources of Passive income or part-time occupation or skill work, in order to supplement their income. It may look difficult, once you start earning your passive income or addl. Source of income, you will forget about the hardship and initial troubles.

Midterm financial goals are achievable with proper allocation of suitable investment options and selecting the right kind of asset classes at the right time, as early as possible.

The investment plan should clearly earmark funds for each type of asset which is aligned to the time frame and corresponding to your deadline. There should not be any suspicion or doubt regarding the achievement of the goal on the specific date.

The goal has to be written on a paper with the photo and with all details and it should be digested and captured by your subconscious mind every day, so that your determination to achieve the goal will become stronger and stronger, and you will somehow find out the golden key to open the doors of fortune, to make the dream reality.

Do not underestimate the capacity of your inner mind, your untapped powers and energies, which are going to be magically connected to your dominant single desire and wavelengths of your daily affirmations.

5. Review and Replan Your loans and Advances portfolio:

The biggest advantage of the Technology is that anything can be done quickly and without much effort, with the comfort of your Mobile or other gadgets. On the other side of the coin, we will also become victims of negative factors with the same speed and without our knowledge.

The credit card apps or loans apps are a boon to the people who need quick loans or advances with the comfort of online processing and on a virtual platform within a short time.

At the same time, we never realize the crippling impact of their interest burden or perpetual debt trap of these well marketed vicious loans.

Many people never come out of the vicious circle of debt trap of these credit cards or Private lenders, as these people are ever ready to respond to your request for loans, and they entice you with attractive offers and ease of processing.

But, once you are in the clutches of these big loan sharks, you will be bleeding forever, unable to get out of these crippling habit of borrowing with interest rates of 48% to 60% per annum.

Exiting or closing the high interest loans is one of the important steps in prudential financial planning and if not possible, exploring the option of shifting to some other take over loans, with lesser interest options.

Any person who wishes to meet the financial goals should have a complete knowledge of how the credit card billing cycle works and how to use the credit card to the optimum use, to use the free credit period etc.

6. COVERING THE life RISKS AND shifting the loss of unexpected loss of life, health etc.

Taking Term insurance for Life Risk and Planning for children's education or settlement etc is part of financial planning.

Risk protection is the important factor, which can not be postponed at all, if you want to protect yourself from the risk of loss of health, loss of income etc.

7. Tax planning and tax-free investment products planning:

Financial planning for life goals

The importance of personal financial planning in India cannot be ignored. It is not just about increasing your savings and reducing your expenses. Financial planning is a lot more than that. This includes achieving your future goals, such as:

1. *Wealth creation*

   The rise in the price of everyday items means that if you want to maintain or increase your current standard of living in the future, you need to create a sufficient corpus of wealth. You may also want to purchase a better car or a new house in the future. All this requires money, and it merely highlights the importance of wealth creation. It is possible to achieve these goals by carefully investing your money in the right avenues. Equity mutual funds can be a suitable option for long term goals. These funds could help the investor to accumulate wealth in the long run.

2. *Retirement planning*
   Your retirement may be 25 or 30 years in the future. But that does not mean you plan for it when you retire. To enjoy a happy and comfortable retired life, you need to start building your safety net right now. Planning at an early stage in life can help secure your future against financial uncertainties. Also, you invest lesser amounts if you start early and gain from the power of compounding, which helps to build a large enough corpus over the 25-30 year period.
3. *Child's education* has become very expensive, not only in India but across the world. And in future, this cost is only going to rise. This is why it is necessary to start planning from the moment your child is born. Calculate how much you wish to earn and start investing in long-term investment avenues that can help you achieve this goal. You can approach a financial advisor for advice if you are not sure how to proceed further.

4.Saving tax

Every year, you are probably paying a substantial amount as tax. But you can now lower your tax outgo legally. The Indian Income Tax Act provides various provisions for people to reduce their tax outgo. By planning your taxes in advance, you can identify the best avenues to invest your money and reduce your taxable income. Mutual funds provide a tax efficient avenue for investing for your life goals.

The first step before considering a Financial Product is to understand the Risk appetite, risk aptitude, Risk capacity of the investor.

Second factor is time ... required for executing the plan.

Similarly, each investment should go through some basic filters or checkpoints in order to be eligible for investment, generally:

What are the basic principles of any Investment:

Safety:

Safety of our capital or whatever we have invested is of the utmost importance and under no circumstances, there should not be any capital erosion or threat to the capital invested by us. This is the basic and fundamental principle of any investment. Whenever we are planning to invest the amount, we have to think of this factor as a prerequisite whether to proceed further or not.

Whenever it is perceived to be risky even to the capital invested, we have to think twice before proceeding further. Liquidity:

Liquidity means how fast we can convert an investment into cash or how fast we can sell the investment in the market and get back our investment. It is a very important factor. Suppose we are thinking of buying a land in a remote rural area and where there is a less possibility of more demand for such types of land, it is called illiquid asset, as in case of emergency or in case we want to sell the property, there would not be any buyers for such type of land or Real estate.

Similarly, whenever we are thinking of any investment, we have to think of the market lot or size of the marketable lot and whether we can sell part of the property or there is no chance of dividing it to smaller ones. Whenever there is a possibility of selling smaller units which are more affordable to more people the property is more liquid than a property which can not be cut into pieces.

What is the minimum period of holding of any property or whether there is a mandatory holding period or not has to be taken into account. This is called Lock in period. For example, if you invest in Tax Savings Bank Fixed Deposits, You can not sell them or take any loan against them, until 5 years. In other words, the investment lock in period is 5 years and you can not touch that investment during the lock in period. Lesser the lock in period the better would be the demand for such types of Investments.

Any expenditure or Load at the time of selling or redemption: Some Investments demand some sort of Penalty or load, at the time of sale or redemption, when the investor tries to sell the investment, before maturity date. That is called Premature cancellation charges in Banks and exit load in the Stock market. One has to take into account these expenses, while considering the liquidity aspect.

Returns:

As seen earlier in the definition of investments, the major purpose is to get some returns from investment. Such returns may be in the form of regular (or periodic) income, also known as current income; and capital appreciation, or capital gains.

The current income is receivable periodically, without having to sell the investment,

whereas, the capital gains can be realized only when one sells the investment.

The exit charges, or penalty, would bring down the returns, as seen earlier. Hence, whenever there are any such charges for early withdrawals, the same must be considered as a trade-off between liquidity and returns.

Convenience:

Any investment must be evaluated in terms of convenience with respect to investing, taking the money out–fully or partially, as well as the investor's ability to conveniently check the value of the investment, as well as to receive the income.

Ticket size:

What is the minimum amount required for investment? There are some avenues where an investor can start investing amounts as small as Rs. 50 or Rs. 100, whereas some require more than Rs. 1 lakh, and sometimes more than Rs. 1 crore. This becomes an important factor while taking a decision about selection of investment options. At the same time, this must not be the only factor. Some investors (though a very small number) have started considering certain investments (requiring large amounts), only because they could afford the same, without checking whether they needed it, or if that was appropriate for their situation and need.

Taxability of income:

What one retains after taxes is what matters, and hence, taxation of the earnings is another important factor that one must consider. While looking at the taxability of income, it is critical to evaluate various other factors, too, and not look at taxation in isolation. For example, some products may offer lower tax on investment returns, but the safety also may be low.

1. Start early as soon as you start earning. The earlier, better.
2. Go for good and fundamentally strong stocks thru Mutual fund route.

****

CHAPTER FIVE

WHAT IS MUTUAL FUND?

- **It is formed by putting together a group of investors who pool in their money, and the investment is done by a professional fund house for a fee through its professional fund managers.**
- **In order to accommodate various investors' preferences, mutual funds mobilize different pools of money. Each such pool of money is called a '*Mutual Fund Scheme*'.**
- **Every scheme has a pre-announced investment objective. When investors**

invest in a mutual fund scheme, they are effectively buying into its investment objective. The objective can be to invest in Equity, Debt, Gold

or it can be to invest in all of them together through various hybrid schemes.

<u>The NAV is equivalent to:</u>

Unit-holders' Funds in the Scheme (Net Assets) ÷ No. of Units

Which effectively implies that:

- Higher the interest, dividend and capital gains earned by the scheme, higher would be the NAV.
- Higher the appreciation in the investment portfolio, higher would be the NAV.
- Lower the expenses, higher would be the NAV.

Systematic Investment Plan (SIP)

- SIP is an approach where the investor invests constant amounts at regular intervals.
- A benefit of such an approach, particularly in equity schemes, is that it averages the unit-holder's cost of acquisition.
- AMC's have provided a facility to increase SIP amount every year (SIP Top up) e.g. SIP initially created for Rs.2000/-p.m. will increase by specified amount say 10% every year so the SIP next year would be Rs.2200/-p.m.

Systematic Withdrawal Plan (SWP)

With this facility, Investors can opt for the safer route of offering for re-purchase, a constant value of units /amount over a period of time. It is just the reverse of SIP.

Dematerialization is a process whereby an investor's holding of investments in physical form (paper), is converted into a digital record. The benefit of holding investments in Demat form:

- Less paperwork in buying or selling the Units
- Direct credit of bonus and rights units that the investor is entitled
- Change of address or other details need to be updated only to the Depository Participant.

Consolidate all investments in mutual funds, direct equity, debentures, and others under one account,

If you have the interest and inclination and time to understand the stocks, the business cycles, and other financial ratios, and willing to learn and experiment, start with a reputed Mutual funds, which is consistently giving good dividends, for the last 5 years and start reading all the financial reports of the portfolios etc.

1. **Once, you gain enough experience and knowledge about markets, decide on the stocks to be purchased, which are consistently growing and which are of market leaders. Try to acquire them in small lots, whenever there is a dip in the market. Do it systematically, every month, so that market ups and downs will not effect you.**
2. Always go for the long run, not short run.Have a detailed statement of purpose and your financial goals, why you are investing in that particular asset. So think for long term. Never enter into the stock market, for short term gains or for short tenure. Wealth creation never happens in short term.
3. Go for index funds, if you are not comfortable with market volatility or your knowledge is not adequate to pick up right stocks. The easiest way of picking of stocks is to follow the Sensex or Nifty fifty / index stocks, which are market leaders and follow the same portfolio and same strategy of buying or selling the stocks as per the Index. Ultimately,no sensex or No nifty fifty index falls over a long period.
4. Rupee cost averaging: The advantage of systematic Investment Plan is your average cost of investment will be less by Rupee cost averaging over a period of time. Irrespective of market ups and downs, you have to invest a fixed amount every month either thru SIP or in stocks, so that your cost of acquisition of the stock is getting lowered over a period of time.
5. Power of compounding.

Power of compounding is the magic and you will not realise it, until, you experience it. Even a small investment of Rs.5000/ every month will make you a correpati, over a period of 20 to 25 years, basing on the average compound return of 15 to 20% per Annum. Those who would like to create wealth, should select a good asset class, which beats inflation, and start investing everymonth consistently, without bothering about market fluctuations.

Investment planning advantages:

The main objectives of your investment planning or strategy:

- **BEAT THE INFLATION.**

As long as your return on investment is below the inflation rate, you are becoming poorer day by day. Your intrinsic value of your investment is getting eroded over a period of time. Hence, avoid investment in any type of investment, where the return is below the rate of inflation.

- **CONSTANTLY COMPARE YOUR RATE OF RETURN ON YOUR INVESTMENTS AND COST OF INFLATION.**

OTHERWISE, YOUR investment will get a negative return.

Financial planning is a step-by-step approach to meet one's life goals. A financial plan acts as a guide as you go through life's journey. Essentially, it helps you be in control of your income, expenses and investments such that you can manage your money and achieve your goals.

If you take a closer look at the above examples, you'll find that there is one factor that connects all of them: money. You need to have an adequate amount of money to fulfil your goals and desires. More importantly, you need to have money at the right point in time.

For example, if you want to build up a corpus of Rs. 10 lakh for your daughter's college education through investments, you need to grow this amount by the time she turns 18. Not a year later. This is where financial planning becomes essential.

What are the Benefits of Financial planning?

There are numerous practical benefits to financial planning. It helps you to:

1. Increase your savings
   It may be possible to save money without having a financial plan. But it may not be the most efficient way to go about it. When you create a financial plan, you get a good deal of insight into your income and expenses. You can track and cut down your costs consciously. This automatically increases your savings in the long run.
2. Enjoy a better standard of living
   Most people assume that they would have to sacrifice their standard of living if their monthly bills and EMI repayments are to be addressed. On the contrary, with a good financial plan, you would not need to compromise your lifestyle. It is possible to achieve your goals while living in relative comfort.
3. Be prepared for emergencies
   Creating an emergency fund is a critical aspect of financial planning. Here, you need to ensure that you have a fund that is equal to at least 6 months of your monthly salary. This way, you don't have to worry about procuring funds in case of a family emergency or a job loss. The emergency fund can help you pay for varied expenses on time.
4. Attain peace of mind
   With adequate funds at hand, you can cover your monthly expenses, invest for your future goals and splurge a little for yourself and your family, without worry. Financial planning helps you manage your money efficiently and enjoy peace of mind. Don't worry if you have not yet reached this stage. If you are on the path of financial planning, the destination of financial peace is not very far away.

The importance of personal financial planning in India cannot be ignored. It is not just about increasing your savings and reducing your expenses. Financial planning is a lot more than that. This includes achieving your future goals, such as:

1.

   Every year, you are probably paying a substantial amount as tax. But you can now lower your tax outgo legally. The Indian Income Tax Act provides various provisions for people to reduce their tax outgo. By planning your taxes in advance, you can identify the best avenues to invest your money and reduce your taxable income. Mutual funds provide a tax efficient avenue for investing for your life goals.

Why is personal financial planning crucial?

- ***To tackle inflation***

Remember the time you went to a multiplex with your family. You must have probably heard your grandparents say: 'Everything was so cheap back then'. It's true. Twenty years ago, the cost of movie tickets was around Rs. 40, not Rs. 500 as it is today. Similarly, chocolates, coffee, clothes, petrol and other regular goods were much cheaper 'back then'. This phenomenon of prices rising over the years is known as inflation. It is the steady increase in the price of goods and services over time. And if you are not careful, it can eat into your savings in no time. Here's a simple example to illustrate its effect.

Imagine a chocolate bar costs Rs. 10 today, and you have Rs. 100. With this amount, you can buy 10 chocolate bars. Over the next one year, imagine you keep Rs. 100 in a bank that offers you an annual interest rate of 5%. At the end of the year, you have Rs. 105 with you.

But over one year, let's assume that the price of the chocolate bar increases to Rs. 11. This means you have to pay Rs. 110 to purchase the same 10 chocolate bars next year. But since you have only Rs. 105, you fall short of Rs. 5. This is how inflation eats into one's savings. It reduces purchasing power over time, and you have to pay more money to buy the same goods.

You can combat inflation by investing in avenues that offer you better returns over time. But for this, financial planning is critical.

- **To create a contingency fund**

The future is uncertain, and anything can happen at any time. Here's a scenario that highlights this point.

Imagine a father who has taken an education loan to finance his daughter's college education. At the same time, he is also saving money to fund his retirement that is a couple of years away. But suddenly, a medical emergency occurs in the family. Unfortunately, the lack of medical insurance coverage means he has to pay for medical expenses out of his savings. This depletes his retirement corpus and increases his financial burden.

Many people face such situations. And while it is good to hope for the best, it is necessary to plan for the worst. A sudden job loss or an unexpected medical emergency can shake up your finances considerably. This is why you need to have an emergency fund to deal with such issues. Financial experts advise investors to keep an amount equal to 6 months' salary as a contingency fund. This can be invested in a liquid fund so that you can access the money quickly in case of an emergency.

- **To create a retirement corpus**

Newer medicines and more significant advances in the medical field mean that people are now living longer retired lives. This is undoubtedly a good thing. You can enjoy more time with your family, explore your passions and dreams, and travel around the world. But there's one crucial question you need to consider: how can I fund all these expenses? You need to have an adequate amount of money to ensure you enjoy your retired life to the fullest. This is possible by having a financial plan that provides regular income post retirement.

- **To manage your money in the best possible manner**

Satisfying the needs of your family members can be tricky. Your teenage son may want to go to a space camp during the summer, while your oldest child is ready to go to college. In personal finance, planning is vital. It not only helps you understand the needs of different family members, but also how you can achieve them. But for this, you need to manage your money in the best possible manner.

For instance, parking your savings in a bank account is better than spending all of it. However, this is not the best way to deploy your money. In comparison, avenues like mutual funds could provide better annual yields. So, when you identify your family's needs and make your money work actively to achieve them, you may expect to see good results.

How to create a successful financial plan?

1. **Understand your current financial situation**
   determine the status of your current finances, viz., your income, expenses, debt, savings and investments. This is the first step in financial planning, as it gives you a good sense of the state of your finances and ways to improve.
2. **Write down your financial goals,**
   Ask yourself: 'what are the different financial goals I wish to achieve in life?' Write them on a piece of paper. Don't hesitate to put down any goal because no goal is too small or too big. However, make sure that your goals are specific. For instance, here are some achievable goals: 'I want to purchase an SUV worth Rs. 13 lakh in the next 18 months' or 'I want to buy a flat worth Rs. 80 lakh in the next 5 years.
3. **Look at the different investment options**
   There are numerous investment options available to investors. In the mutual fund market alone, you can choose from nearly 2,000 schemes. Different investment avenues help investors to achieve different goals. For example, equity funds are suitable

for long-term goals like retirement planning, child's education, etc. If you are interested in relatively steady income, and you are risk averse, you may want to invest in debt mutual funds. Equity Linked Saving Scheme (ELSS fund) is good to save tax. When it comes to investing, many financial experts have highlighted the importance of mutual funds. Investing in these funds consistently over a longer period can help you achieve your dreams and goals.

4. **Implement the right plan**
   You need to select the right investment option based on factors such as your goals, age, risk appetite and investment amount. If you are unsure on the funds you need to select for your portfolio, you can avail the services of a financial advisor. These are certified professionals who help investors make the right investment choices. They also help with other aspects like insurance, retirement planning, estate planning and taxation.
5. **Monitor your financial plan**
   The financial planning process does not end once you invest your money. You also need to monitor how the funds are performing regularly. If they don't perform, you may need to replace them with better-performing funds. You also need to follow your plan because as you grow older, your goals and dreams evolve. For instance, your financial priorities may change after the birth of a child. Now, you need to accommodate the expenses and objectives of a new member in your family.

****

CHAPTER SIX

HOW TO START MY JOURNEY?

Who is my guide, or where is my road map?

some Basic fundamental concepts of Investment:

simple interest is the interest that gets paid only on the outstanding principal

Compound interest is paid on both interest and the principal outstanding

Interest and return are like two sides of the same coin

Absolute return is a measure of the growth in return when your investment if for less than a year

Compounded annual growth rate (CAGR) is the measure of your return when your investment duration is more than a year

Compounding works best when you give your investments enough time to grow

1.

How to start? Where is the detailed action plan?

Once you prepare your financial goals and present a financial position sheet, you have to start immediately ... i.e. the earlier, the better.

Many people are under the impression that retirement planning or planning for a rainy day is for the Middle aged or for those who are going to retire in the next few years. It is widely believed that people have to enjoy it at a younger age irrespective of its cost and repercussions.

How much money should I have at retirement? – Retirement Planning

The key point behind successful retirement planning is ensuring the retirement fund to be large enough to meet all the retirement needs. For that, retirement needs have to be identified and properly quantified.

As shown in the info-gram provided below the most obvious retirement needs include:

1. **Ensuring a steady income**
2. **meeting health-related expenses and**
3. **maintaining the lifestyle.**

Life events or stages, how to plan for the stage

There are several life stages. If you have clear idea of various stages of life and their potential demands of money, you should realised the importance of planning for future and life changing needs.

Life stages:

a. **Youth ..Spending and no savings stage**
b. **Married... needs are mounting and income is not sufficient**
c. **Married with kids... Responsibilities are mounting**
d. **Middle aged. With adult children... settlement time**
e. **Children at marriageable age... worried years**
f. **Retired.. should be peaceful**

Some of the available popular plans for retirement corpus or retirement planning in India.

1. **NPS – National Pension System**

National pension system or NPS is a Government sponsored pension scheme where voluntary contributions and their investment returns are accumulated into a pension fund managed by fund managers. The pension fund is invested in annuity schemes designed by insurance companies later on to provide a steady annuity. Read complete details on National Pension System (NPS) and its tax implications.

1. **PPF – Public Provident Fund**

Public provident fund is another popular Government sponsored savings scheme where the applicable interest rate is declared on a quarterly basis. This is a 15-year scheme which can be extended further in five-year blocks thereafter. Maximum deposit allowed is 1,50,000 per annum. Payments towards PPF account, interest received and the withdrawn amount from the account is exempted from income tax. Read all the details on Public Provident Fund (PPF) you need to know.

3. **Jeevan Shanti (Table 850) Pension scheme from LIC or any comparable annuity scheme by Insurance schemes**

Jeevan Shanti from LIC of India is a deferred/immediate annuity plan which can be used to invest the pension fund. Jeevan Shanti provides guaranteed life long pension with umpteen options to customize pension received. Jeevan Shanti provides insurance coverage also during the deferment period. Read complete details of Jeevan Shanti plan with pension calculators.

4. **Atal Pension Yojana**

Atal Pension Yojana (previously known as Swavalamban Yojana) is a government-backed pension scheme in India targeted at the unorganized sector. People below the age of 40 are eligible for a pension of up to Rs.5,000 per month on the attainment of 60 years of age.

The consumerist behaviour pattern promoted and marketed by MNCs and colourfully depicted in the social media will prompt the young generation in instant gratification and the aping of western culture, which will have a devastating impact on life in the coming years.

Hence, start as early as possible once you start earning, and it will drastically reduce your burden later. It doesn't mean that you should live a miserable life and should not enjoy the good things of life. It means regulating your desires and not denial. Once you have a clear-cut financial goal and time horizon to achieve it, you have to control your desires and commit to your goal right from a young age, so that you have a healthy financial discipline to enjoy life in later years with the power of financial independence.

Similarly, the protection needs of Life Insurance and Health Insurance should also be planned from early life, so that the cost of insuring for unknown perils will be very low, and you will have a comfortable journey, even, in the event of some unforeseen risk of hospitalization or accidents.

2. *Whom to follow? Is it reliable or trustworthy?*

In India, Financial literacy is woefully very low.

No college or Institution will teach the subject, how to face the real life and life adverse situations. Most adverse situations, like loss of job or income, sudden sickness of self or relatives ...require a lot of financial support and courage.

Hence, Pl follow a top Mutual Fund which is giving a reasonable return consistently and with a good diverse large cap stock allocation. It is indirectly easy to enter into the stock market, through some experienced Fund Manager. Instead of putting a large lump sum amount, you can start with a small amount of Rs. 1000/- per month to test the waters.

You can also invest some amount in some index fund which imitates or mimics some market index like NIFTY FIFTY or BSE Sensex, where the returns or reasonable and volatility is comparatively less.

Don't ever try to have 100% risk-free investments, in the early age, which will compromise your return, and you may end up getting negative returns.

Having said that, I never suggest you that you have to ignore the real estate or Gold investments, which are also to be considered to some extent, subject to certain risks.

But any person, who wishes to accumulate wealth over a period of time, should always select an asset, which should beat the inflation and which should be able to build a corpus over a longer period. If you want to get income, you can trade in the stocks, but if you want wealth, there is no other asset, which will give you a better return than equity.

But investing in stocks or direct equity is not that easy. It requires a lot of skill, knowledge and patience to pick up good industries, sectors and stocks. It requires a lot of interest, focus and time to have a grip on the market

Especially for a retail investor, it is very dangerous and risky to enter directly into the stock market. He may lose his entire capital or he may not be able to get any return also, without having proper knowledge.

Hence, for a layman and a beginner, it is always preferable to enter into the equity market in an indirect manner, i.e. through Mutual Fund houses and with SIP(systematic Investment Plan) which will give the advantage of rupee compounding and price average benefits.

Whether the stock market is in an upward direction or downward direction,the investor is going to get benefit over a longer period, through SIP transactions.

3.

What is a portfolio? How to select the investment basket?

The term portfolio investments covers a wide range of asset classes including stocks, government bonds, corporate bonds, real estate investment trusts (REITs), mutual funds, exchange-traded funds (ETFs), and bank Fixed deposits etc, which are meant for wealth and income creation over a longer period.

The portfolio will be decided by the investors risk capacity, risk appetite, and duration of the investment.

4.

What is the barometer? How to measure success?

The real success of wealth creation or good return is actual average returns over a time period of 5 to 10 years, vis-à-vis market average return or risk free return.

Any return over and above the Bank FD return is considered to be good and any return which multiplies your investment within a short period, is considered to be most successful investment. Whether it is stock investment or Real Estate or any other investment.

5.

What are the various pros and cons?

Generally, wherever there is more risk, there is more reward and return. But, there is higher risk of loosing the capital also.

Hence, the capital protection is more important and at the same time, taking a calculated risk to maximise the returns.

Having a well diversified portfolio, with the aim of risk diversification and selection of investments is the important step for optimisation of returns. But, if you are not taking any risk at all, you may end up eroding your current value of investment also. Money stored in lockers or in cupboards does not grow even a single paisa and there is more risk of theft and spending on unnecessary, non productive things or products.

6.

What is the effect of following the herd ? What is the real fact from the hype?

Most of the people doesn't understand the money or economics. People can not manage their money due to lack of knowledge and fear of safety.

Many people give free advice, without having any idea of risks involved in such type of investments. No two individuals are same. Their needs and capacity of risk bearing is not the same. So investment decisions are taken based on the various relevant factors like risk capacity, duration, available alternatives, liquidity etc. Don't ever follow your relative or friend advice blindly, without considering your individual capacity and limitations.

7.

Do I have to invest? If at all for how much perioid?

Yes. If you want to live a trouble free life and peace of mind, plan for a rainy day. Start early and provide for your probable risks in the future like, health, education of children, safety needs, and lastly retirement corpus.

A systematic investment, will relieve your stress in case of emergency and improves your quality of life over a longer period.

You have to invest as long as you can for your emergencies and future plans.

please remember.....

Investing for a rainy day, if not for wealth creation, is mandatory and saves a person from future emergencies.

****

CHAPTER SEVEN

WHERE IS OUR ROAD MAP? WHAT ARE OUR MILESTONES?

This is your ROAD MAP, curated by a Financial Adviser.

1.When you are building a house, you are spending some amount for blue print and designs.

Similarly, it is worth spending some money to Qualified and sincere Financial Advisors or Family Brokers, who are known for their knowledge and integrity.

Don't ever do the initial planning by yourself as you are not aware of the tools and various investment schemes, to reach your financial goals.

Not withstanding your professional qualifications, irrespective of your status and name in the society, it is better to learn from some experts, who have the necessary experience in creation of wealth and had the exposure of various storms and ups and downs in the financial world.

2 write down all your Financial goals.

3 keep your execution plan ready.

4 verify whether your goals are mapped to the execution plan

Have a review of the plan, if you have some doubts or the plan may not be practical.

Start implementing the plan as early as possible and making a diary entry

Review the journey, every quarter and take whether the plan is working properly or not.

In the annual review, if there is any negative return or the investment plan is not on expected

Lines, immediately consult your Finacial advisor for mid term corrective action.

START YOUR JOURNEY WITH either SIP OR SWP, AS PER THE PLAN

WHAT IS SIP... SYSTEMATIC INVESTMENT PLAN.

ADVANTAGES OF SIP:

- flexible and we can start with small investment o – You can always start with smaller amounts and increase the sum of investment as your earning grows with time.
- No entry no exit charges – you can go for topup or pause it.
- Saves you time – it can be automated or mandate can be given for recurring SIP amounts,
- No worry about sensex falling or market crashes. Whether in Bull market or bear market, you will win.
- You need not worry about the market conditions or valuations. The systematic plan will take care of averaging of your cost of acquisition and

- It will be compounding interest of the returns over a period of time that makes your journey more exciting.

Keep in Mind

COMPOUND INTEREST - THE EIGHTH WONDER OF THE WORLD

March 14 marks the birth anniversary of renowned physicist Albert Einstein. While the legend is celebrated for his contribution to science, believe it or not, he also has a connection to the wonderland of investment. The seven wonders of the world are known globally today. But decades ago, Einstein regarded compound interest as the eighth wonder of the world. After earning and losing money in the Stock Market, he also said, "He who understands it (compound interest), earns it, he who doesn't, pays it."

If you are middle aged or about to retire shortly, think about your retirement planning and

Life after retirement. Don't expose yourself to risk of equity markets.

Senior citizens Investments opportunities:

1. PF/ WITHDRAWAL... PL. EXTEND FOR 3 YRS 8.5%
2. EMERGENCY FUND: 6 TO 8 MONTHS... LIQUID FUNDS
3. HEALTH INSURANCE : PURCHASE
4. DON'T LOCK YOUR INVESTMENT FOR LONG TERM
5. ANNUITIES, IF PENSION IS NOT THERE
6. PMVV FOR MONTHLY PENSION
7. POST OFFICE... SENIOR CITIZENS SCHEME
8. WE can invest in Debt instruments, which are guaranteed by the Govt or sovereign bonds.

Covered bonds are debt securities issued by a bank or mortgage institution and collateralized against a pool of assets that, in case of failure of the issuer, can cover claims at any point of time. They are subject to specific legislation to protect bondholders.

General perception of risk with various Asset classes and Investments

EQUITY INVESTMENT... FOR RISK TAKERS.. high risk and high return.. generally

BOND / DEBT... NON - risk takers... debt/bonds/ bank FD

BANK FD... 4 to 5% return... post tax return 2 to 3 percent. „upto Rs.5 lakhs no risk. Insurance coverage.

Higher return than Bank FD: debt mutual funds... better return than BANK deposits but more risk than bank deposits, for longer duration.

Step 1:

Invest in Assets not in liability, for the sake of False Prestige.

Never ever acquire an asset that is a liability to you and which is not generating any income for you at an early age. Instead of purchasing a luxury car with 20 lacs, buy a commercial property, which will give you an 8% return.

If you continuously invest the interest amount even in a secured debt @ 9%, you will get back your Rs.20 lakhs within a small period of 8 years.

Become a part owner of Equity or well-managed companies of essential commodities:

However small it is, buy shares of well-performing companies, whose turnover is growing continuously @ 10% year-on-year. Eg. HDFC Bank, HUL, Asian Paints etc.

Even though it appears to be expensive initially, you will become part of their growth story and part of their empire building.

Don't ever repeat the financial investment paths or patterns of your father or grandfather, who have lived a mediocre financial life.

It is not How much income you are earning every month, it is how much you are able to invest... that is the key for your financial growth.

Don't ever borrow from a Credit card or for anything for luxury items or for things that

are not valued for money.

Whenever you are spending any amount, over a longer period-think of whether it is INVESTMENT OR pure expenditure? If the investment is creating value and adding to your wealth or earning capacity, it is an investment. Otherwise, it is nothing but wasteful expenditure making you poorer day by day.

Be regular and systematic. The secret is patience and time. Don't ever look at the market volatility or periodical ups and downs.

Take the cover of your health, wealth, income, reputation and vehicles.

Don't confuse and mix insurance and investment. Always pay the premium for covering the risk but not for getting back your money or multiplying your money.

HAVE a clear understanding of your essentials, needs, comforts and luxuries. Have a budget for a month, a year and for the next five years.

Various Investment choices in stock and other asset classes:

1. Blue Chip Companies
2. Mid-sized companies
3. Small-sized companies
4. Unlisted Companies
5. Foreign Stocks
6. Fixed Income
7. Equity Mutual Funds
8. Exchange Traded Funds
9. Index Funds
10. Fixed deposit with a bank
11. Recurring deposit with a bank
12. Endowment Policies Money back Policies
13. Public Provident Fund
14. Sukanya Samruddhi Yojana (SSY)

15. Senior Citizens' Savings Scheme (SCSS)
16. Post office Monthly Income Scheme
17. Recurring deposit with a post office
18. Company fixed deposit
19. Debentures/bonds
20. Debt Mutual Funds
21. Real Estate/Infrastructure
22. Commodities
23. Physical Asset
24. Residential/ Commercial Financial Asset
25. Real Estate Mutual Funds (REMF)
26. Real Estate Investment Trusts (ReIT)
27. Infrastructure Investment Trust (InvIT)
28. Gold Silver
29. Gold Funds
30. Commodity ETFs
31. Hybrid asset classes
32. Others
33. Hybrid Mutual funds

ALTERNATE INVESTMENTS OR ASSET CLASSES:

1. Rare coins
2. Art
3. Rare stamp
4. CRYPTO currency and other Black chain-supported investments.

Note the difference between active income and passive income. Try to increase your passive income

as early as possible so that your journey will be more comfortable.

Please remember that the future value of money is most important while taking the personal finance decisions.

A bird in hand worth two in the bush. Hence, always protect and invest the money today, instead of waiting for some future date and receiving the same money after a certain future date.

Those who neglect the "time value of money " will not make any wealth.

The value of money today may not the same after 10 years or 15 years. It has got a compounding effect and may grow multiple times. To give an example, the cost of engineering education today is Rs.5 lakhs. But, after 10 years it may go up by either two times or more to 10 lakhs or more.

The compounding effect

Apparently, Albert Einstein once described 'compound interest' as the 8th wonder of the world. I guess he could not describe it any better. To understand why you need to understand the compound interest in conjunction with time.

Compounding in the finance world refers to the ability of money to grow, given that the gains of year 1 get reinvested for year 2, gains of year 2 gets reinvested for year 3, so on and so forth.

For example, consider you invest Rs.100 which is expected to grow at 20% year on year (recall this is also called the CAGR or simply the growth rate). At the end of the first year, the money grows to Rs.120.

At the end of year 1, you have two options –

- Let Rs.20 in profits remain invested along with the original principal of Rs.100 or
- Withdraw the profits of Rs.20

You decide not to withdraw Rs.20 profit; instead, you decide to reinvest the money for the 2nd year. At the end of the 2nd year, Rs.120 grows at 20% to Rs.144. At the end of 3rd year, Rs.144 grows at 20% to Rs.173. So on and so forth.

Compare this with withdrawing Rs.20 profits every year. Had you opted to withdraw Rs.20 every year than at the end of the 3rd year the profits collected would be Rs. 60.

However, since you decided to stay invested, the profits at the end of 3 years are Rs.173/-. This is a good Rs.13 or 21.7% over Rs.60, because you opted to do nothing and decided to stay invested.

This is called the compounding effect.

Always go for growth option in Mutual funds, or Reinvestment plan in Bank FDs, as it has got an advantage of compounding and consistent growth potential, than the regular payout option.

CHAPTER EIGHT

WHEN TO BEGIN? WHAT IS THE RIGHT AGE? START AT THE RIGHT TIME

Old habits die hard. The earlier you start teaching your kids about money, the better it is for moulding their financial personality.

Show them the magic of delayed gratification

Give them one pastry now or a cake later if they wait. This will teach them how curbing their urge now can be crucial for them later.

Let them earn what they want

Pamper your child with love; for money, let them work hard. Reward them a little for doing small chores like cleaning their dishes, making their beds, etc.

Allow them to spend

Ask your kids to make a wish list; give them a certain amount to shop for themselves and tell them to keep whatever remains. They will tend to prioritize their wants and save as much as they can.

Let them have their own investment

You can start a Mutual Fund Systematic Investment Plan (SIP) in your child's name. Since it is their own investment, they will be interested in learning more about it and will also be encouraged to save more.

Birani cited a study that showed that if one invested Rs 25,000 every month in the sensex stocks for 20 years, at the end of the term, going by 15% average annual return compared to sensex's historical compounded annual growth rate (CAGR) of 17%, he would have a corpus of Rs 3.75 crore.

Now if the same amount is invested in FDs, which gives an average annual return of 8%, the total corpus would be about Rs 1.5 crore. "The difference is approximately Rs 2 crore.

This extra savings is the power of compounding from the extra 7% that one could get in equities," he said. ***"One should put money in fixed deposits if you need money in case of an emergency, for meeting expenses during contingencies. For long term asset creation, there are just two asset classes, real estate and equity. To invest in real estate you need a huge amount of money, while to invest in equities, you can start with as little as Rs 500," Birani said.***

Whatever it is, this is the time to tell your reader exactly what they need to do to make the steps they've just taken come to life.

Covid-19 has also irreversibly changed investment patterns, with three big shifts underway. What is now clear is that "black swan" events which were considered to happen once-in-a-generation are now likely to be more frequent.

My own generation has seen three big market meltdowns—

the dotcom bubble in 2001,

he financial crisis in 2008 and

now covid-19.

This means portfolios have to be better positioned to weather these storms. Allocations are now likely to happen at three levels—risk, asset and product—and staying true to one's strategic asset allocation will be the key.

When the dust settles, the society at large will be looking for a better post-covid world. This will drive sustainable and responsible investing by asset owners.

Investing in sound ESG (environmental, social and governance) principles will be the norm rather than the exception.

While 80% of global institutional investing is based on ESG, we have yet to see this trend percolate to individual investment decisions, particularly in India. Covid will accelerate that change and family offices, with larger pools of capital, can play a role in leading the way on responsible investing.

The other shift we will witness is the rise in passive investments (through exchange-traded funds and index funds) and smart beta investing (quant-based strategies), which will provide lower cost of investment. While new to India this is a significant market in the developed countries.

- **"Failing to Plan is Planning to Fail"**

Before the players put on their armours and get on the field, they spend months planning. They understand their areas of improvement, research their opponent and set goals accordingly.

Just like a lot of planning is involved before the matches, investors would also benefit from planning before jumping to invest. They would benefit from identifying their risk appetite, investment potential and setting goals before actual finalising their strategies and assets.

****

CHAPTER NINE

HOW TO ALIGN YOUR FINANCIAL DREAMS TO STRATEGIES?

Ensuring suitability

In order to comply with this basic principle, the investor is required to ensure the scheme's suitability to the his needs and situation.

the asset allocation for the investor is based on the investor's situation and goals.

Therefore, it is a prudent approach to keep the asset allocation at the core of selection of schemes .

Chasing past performance

the mutual fund advertisements use the disclaimer: "Past performance may or may not be sustained in future".

There is a reason for that. As experience has shown time and again, the top performers during one period may not necessarily remain as a top performer forever or near the other top performers and vice versa.

In such a case, simply buying into a scheme due to good returns in the recent past may not be a wise approach.

Understanding the investment objective and investment strategy of the scheme.

In order to evaluate various mutual fund schemes, it is important to consider the scheme's investment objective and strategy.

Both of these can help one understand what to expect from the scheme. Keeping an eye on the taxes and loads, Both taxes and loads reduce investment returns.

Therefore, it is important for the investor to consider these two aspects during repurchases/redemptions. This means that when there is a need to withdraw money from a scheme, the investor must assess the implications of capital gains tax and exit loads.

Likewise, one must also compare the taxation aspects in case of dividend and growth options periodically to evaluate the impact of tax on returns.

Developing a consistent methodology for scheme selection

to have a consistent approach in scheme selection.

It is also important to keep this methodology in writing so that one stays on course

Investment Strategy

The stated Investment objective of the scheme determines the asset class(s) in which it will invest.

IT may be equity, or debt instruments or balanced funds or Real estate, or Bonds.. but the strategy should be mapped to the objective and time horizon of the basic plan. It is most important to realize the goals as per the timeline.

For example, the investment objective to generate capital appreciation in the long term through investment in equity, clearly identifies equity as the asset class in which the scheme will invest.

The Investment strategy of the scheme outlines the approach to be followed in investing the funds to achieve the objective.

This includes factors such as the investment horizon .. to consider when evaluating securities for inclusion in the portfolio, approach to be followed in selecting securities, such as research-based or market-driven,

method of determining the appropriate buying price for the securities,

selling discipline to be followed,

extent of flexibility to be allowed in investing in different asset classes and so on.

We see the world, not as it is, but as we are—or, as we are conditioned to see it."

Have a clear understanding of what are your immediate goals, midterm financial goals and long term goals.

Select your investments, as per your risk perception, investment duration and expected return.

In order to be successful, Financial Planning:

1. **Set SMART - 'Specific, Measurable, Achievable, Relevant, Time-bound' Goals**
2. **Understand the explicit and implicit costs and effects of each financial decision and non-decision**
3. **Periodic review of financial situation and the life goals /objectives is necessary**
4. **Cover all essential areas /aspects of life and explore emerging situations**
5. **Do not procrastinate implementing financial plans or taking any financial decisions**
6. **Be realistic in expectations and make proper assumptions**

****

CHAPTER TEN

REVIEW AND EVALUATION OF TRACK RECORD

"The rich buy assets. The poor only have expenses. The middle class buy liabilities they think are assets"

Robert Kiyosaki..

It is not only the investing in right portfolio, but tracking the investments, and evaluation of performance of the investment is most vital, to reach your goal.

The moment you realize what is an asset and what is a liability, half of your battle is won. You have to shed your ignorance and start comparing yourself with your peers or people in your circle, to think differently and start your journey.

People's lives are forever controlled by two emotions: fear and greed.

Try to control these two emotions. The most important pitfall is following the herd and forgetting to see the reality.

The world is always handing you opportunities of a lifetime, every day of your life, but all too often we fail to see them. We will not reflect or take advantage of our skills and hidden potential. Always the fear, the fear of failure and self-doubt is holding us back to take that first step.

1. Don't ever try to be an employee. Try to provide employment instead.
2. If you want to be rich and wealth, don't ever limit yourself to a 9 to 5 job or some petty job which is providing you some basic needs. You are limiting yourself to the comfort of your job and you will never grow out of it. Even though, there is a risk in the business or profession, try to embrace the risk and try to explore the unknown. You will succeed and realise your real worth. Never settle for mediocracy.

."If you want to move to a higher level of life, you have to be willing to let go of some of your old ways of thinking and being and adopt new ones". T harvEker

1. Understand the power of compounding . Start investing from the day you have started earning. Invest in Assets and not in liabilities.

Upto the age of 45.. live a minimialist life not a miser life. Don't accumulate the material or goods, which are not important or used by you. Don't ever be in the trap of false prestige.

Don't own the things which are capital intensive. Better take on lease if available. Whether it is furniture or machines or anything which is capital intensive.

Don't waste your time and money trying to be master of everything. Instead focus on your core capability and try to utilize it for your development and increase your value. Invest in your skill development, which will in turn improves your ability to earn more and acquire better position or wealth.

Never delay investing. Investment delay cost is very high. Start as early as possible.

If you start early, by the time you are 45 years of age, you need not work harder and live a life of multi-millionaire and have the cake and eat it too. The main secret is starting early and not quitting in the mid-way.

Start improving your knowledge and skills in investment in businesses which are recession proof and which are essentials. If possible, invest in companies which are leaders in the market and where they are having consistent return of more than 15% pa and where the management is not dishonest.

****

CHAPTER ELEVEN

SUMMARY

How to make money in India? OR precisely become rich and a billionaire?

Sensex has delivered 15.5% CAGR returns over last 40 years.

ALL major MUTUAL FUNDS have delivered a return of AROUND 20%.

Having figured out the reasons to invest, the next obvious question would be – Where would one invest, and what are the returns one could expect by investing.

When it comes to investing, one has to choose an **asset class** that suits the

individual's risk and return temperament.

An asset class is a category of investment with particular risk and return characteristics. The following are some of the popular asset classes.

1. Fixed income instruments
2. Equity
3. Real estate
4. Commodities (precious metals)
5. Starting your own business, or entrepreneurial journey

But, Equity investment with proper understanding of the business and markets is the best way to become billionaire in shortest possible time. But it is not everybody's cup of tea. You need to have better grip on economy, proper understanding of economic and political events, global economic trends and wider knowledge of market trends and global opportunities.

IT IS NOW OR NEVER:

IT IS RIGHT TIME TO BECOME BILLINAAIRE NOW, THAN EVER BEFORE, THRU SELECTION OF RIGHT BUSINESSES AND PARTICIPATE IN THEIR GROWTH.

As per the famous Investment adviser Mr. Saurabh Mukherjea, FRSA, founder and Chief Investment Officer of Marcelleus Investment Managers firm,

"Four times in the last 40 years, a US recession alongside falling US bond yields and falling oil prices has been followed by a strong economic recovery in India.

In fact, India has NEVER witnessed an economic recovery without a US recession preceding it!

Now, all three conditions for an Indian economic recovery –

- ***a US recession,***
- ***smashed crude prices and***
- ***falling US Government bond yields are – in place.***

Now the situation is very well suitable for strong economic recovery for the next 5 to 6 years, where high quality management companies will compound their wealth and consolidate their position as market leaders, because of their high and consistent growth for a longer duration, and their technological and higher allocation of capital for the expansion of their business. Economic events or political events does not impact their performance and they are least bothered about the market fluctuations.

Mr. Saurab Mukhejea has quoted the examples of Bajaj Finance, which has tremendous growth of 33% over the last decade.

"Over the past decade (FY11-21) Bajaj Finance (BAF) has grown its loan book at a CAGR of 35% and PAT at a CAGR of 33% with an average RoE of 20%.

During this period credit growth in the Indian banking sector has been only 10% p.a.

BAF has transformed itself from being largely a captive vehicle financier to India's most diversified NBFC which now offers over 40 lending products and has established housing finance and broking subsidiaries. "

Those who have invested one lakh Rupees in the year 2011 has increased their wealth by

How many times? Just see..

The Bajaj Finance company share price as on July 27th July 2012 : Rs. 100 1,00,000

As on June 2022 Rs.6,000/= 60,00,000

Or Rs. One lakh became Rs. Sixty lakhs over a short period of 10 years.

Similarly, Eicher Motors which was at below Rs.200 per share in July 2012 is now trading at Rs. 3000/ per share. @ 1500% growth over a decade.

If you could able to spot such opportunities of 10 companies like that. Do you have the skill and knowledge to identify such companies even now.

Yes. It is possible even now, if you are ready to spare the time and focus on the right parameters and filter the good performing business for your wealth generation.

What is Filter-based approach, and criteria for selection of such multi baggers:

Plase go thru the NIFTY list of top 50 companies and sort them in the order of

a.Their revenue growth over a last decade.

Please sort them on the descending order of their Revenue growth, which should be minimum 15 % Year on Year continuously.

b.Please again filter them based on their return on capital and their capacity to generate free cash flows.

c.Again filter them whether they are able to increase their market value consistently or not over a period of 10 years.

After this triple filters and refinement, you may get around 20 companies or less,

Which satisfies the criteria.

Don't get mislead by their size or turnover or volumes'.

Out of the shortlisted stocks, select the stocks, which are mostly essential goods,

Which are recession proof and which can easily transfer the higher cost of production to the consumer, without any difficulty.

In the post Pandemic era, India is going to witness great economic revival, with the higher local consumption and increased disposable income of the younger generation, who are ready to grab the global opportunities.

No FIIs or No MNC companies can dictate the terms to India, as the economy is matured and our own consumption itself is sufficient to fuel the growth in the stock markets. No more volatility due to the sudden exit of Foreign Institutional Investors or foreign Direct Investments.

Due to formalisation of economy, introduction of GST, adoption of digital economy, India is going to be the fastest Growing economy and all the financial compaies, Banks and NBFCs will definitely benefit from the growing consolidation of the leaders of the industry and continued support of local investors.

Please keep in mind that ...

While investing in such corporates...

1 Promoter should not be dishonest

2. The product is essential

3. The barrier to entry is very high.

The most shocking revelation is... 70% of the stocks in Nifty50 never generated any free cash inflow for the last 10 years.

There is no correlation between sales and profit. To take an example, in the Airline Industry, and in Telecom Industry, always the volume of sales is generally growing at more than 30% per annum.

In spite of the increase in the sale of Airline tickets, no Airline is making profit or at least showing any free cash flow in their balance sheets.

It happened with JET airways, Spicejet, Indian airlines etc.

The same is the case with Bharti Airtel, Vodaphone etc..

Every year the sales or Turnover or Revenue growth will increase by 20% or 30% but it is not getting reflected in the Profit growth or cash flow or reflected in the value of the stock.

No analyst or Fund Manager generally reveal this vital weakness in their fact sheets or risk factors, and people are getting carried away by the fancy ads, highlights of positive factors etc only, so that the common man get convinced about the growth, and enter into the market with a very high valuation bubble, which will burst on any day.

If you can discover such type of stock which is like Asian paints, then you will get double digit capital appreciation and as well as consistent return over a long term.

More and More younger generation will enter into the stock market and increase in the financial assets will increase the wealth of the investors, who will avail this opportunity now.

In the last 10 years, there has been a tremendous transformation of Indian business, which can be attributed to the following infrastructure push.

1. Broadband connectivity
2. Road connectivity
3. UPI & Aadhar
4. GST ..rollout
5. Availability of Cheap but powerful technologies

Only a few business houses could able to make use of these initiatives and improve their wealth and free cash flows.

India is not the USA. What works in the US may not be applicable in India.

It is not sales growth, it is not P/E ratios or it is not Profit after Tax,(PAT) which is going to decide the price of a share or success of a business.

It is the ability to sustain the revenue growth year after year or generate huge free cash flow in the business and how efficiently they are able to use the technology, that divides the class from the mass.

It is no secret that in India, only 20 big corporates account for 80% of profits in this year, whether covid or no covid situation. They are the people who don't steal the public money, who doesn't cook their Balance sheets, and who have not yet become complacent in improving their rank.

Only those who understand the underlying dynamics of the economy only can create wealth and become Titans of Industry.

Typical fixed income investment includes:

1. Fixed deposits offered by banks.
2. Bonds issued by the Government of India
3. Bonds issued by Government related agencies such as HUDCO, NHAI, etc
4. Bonds issued by corporate's

When an investor invests in equity, unlike a fixed income instrument, there is no capital guarantee. However, as a trade-off, the returns from equity investment can be handsome. Indian Equities have generated returns close to 14% – 15% CAGR (compound annual growth rate) over the past 15 years.

Investing in some of the best and well run Indian companies has yielded over 20% CAGR in the long-term. Identifying such investment opportunities requires skill, hard work, and patience.

Taxation on Equity investments held for more than 365 days is taxed at 10%, if the gains are more than Rs 1 lakh starting from 1st April 2018(previously such investments were tax-free). This is comparatively a lower rate of tax than the other asset classes.

a.FAVOURITE STOCKS OF MUTUAL FUND COMPANIES:

1. RELIANCE
2. L&T
3. SBI
4. AXIS BANK
5. BHARTI AIRTEL
6. INFOSYS
7. HDFC BANK
8. ICICI BANK

b.MY FAVOURITES:

1 ASIAN PAINTS
2.PIDILITE
3.HDFC BANK
4.HUL
5.ITC
6.NESTLE
7.TCS
8.INFOSYS
9.L&T
10. TATA MOTORS.

c.**MONOPOLY STOCKS IN INDIA.**

1. IRCTC (100%)

1. HAL(AVIATION)100%
2. NESTLE(CERELAC)96.5%
3. COAL INDIA(82%)

Caution:

Direct investment in equity market is highly risky and it requires lot of knowledge and mental ability to take right decisions and to manage the volatility. Those who are otherwise busy and impatient, does not have the necessary skills and knowledge should never invest their money directly in stock market, looking at some inspiring stories in the media, or some advice from friends or relatives.

It is better to test the waters, through indirect route, thru Mutual funds and improving the knowledge of various types of investments before, directly investing either thru online platform or thru direct equity investments.

But please bear in mind that Past performance is not the indication of future performance and it is not an investment advice by me. It is only for education and knowledge purpose.

Any person, who would like to invest in stock market either directly or indirectly should assess their risk capacity and aptitude and do their **due diligence, before taking any investment decision.**

Real Estate Investments:

Real Estate Investment involves transacting (buying and selling) commercial and non-commercial land. Typical examples would include transacting in sites, apartments and commercial buildings. There are two income sources from real estate investments, namely – Rental income, and Capital appreciation of the investment amount.

The transaction procedure can be quite complex involving legal verification of documents. The cash outlay in real estate investment is usually quite large.

Commodity – Bullion

Investments in gold and silver are considered one of the most popular investment avenues. Gold and silver over a long-term period have appreciated. Investments in these metals have yielded a CAGR return of approximately 8% over the last 20 years. There are several ways to invest in gold and silver.

The evidence suggests that many people save too little, others make poor investment decisions, and others spend their accumulated assets too quickly in retirement.

The 'behavioural' reasons for such tendencies include overconfidence, limited self-control, overvaluation of the present at the expense of the future, framing and loss aversion biases.

<u>INVESTMENT IN CRYPTO CURRENCY</u>?

What if Interest is paid out weekly and you have the liberty to withdraw any amount at any time while you earn interest, that too without any penalty.

WHAT IF ...If you get the assurance of more than 12% interest, which is calculated daily and paid out weekly?

What if... if interest is compounded every week, instead of every quarter or every year?

Yes. It appears that it is too good to be true, in the present FD rates scenario globally and in the present taxation rules.

But wait.... Don't jump to conclusion....

Vexed by the poor interest on bank FDs (0 to 1% PA) in US / Europe/Japan, now the investors of these advanced nations are directing their funds to Crypto currencies, like Bitcoins/Ethereum etc and other popular crypto coins for investment/lending/ trading.. even though with a bit of Risk.

But, they are ready to take the plunge, prepared to take the risk and minting money literally.

The trend is catching and spreading like a wild fire and becoming viral in India also, and going by the attractiveness of this Crypto currency, the neo rich and young millennials are ready to jump in and they are not worried about the inherent risk factors or volatility.

Some of the private sector banks are promoting this trend and no Central Bank is in a position to control the trend.

Is it a indication of probable end of financial intermediation of the traditional banking system? And start of new disrupting virtual currency and exchange system.. the change is very fast and it may be next big innovation by block chain...

A cryptocurrency is a medium of exchange that is digital, encrypted and decentralized. Unlike the U.S. Dollar or the Euro, there is no central authority that manages and maintains the value of a cryptocurrency. Instead, these tasks are broadly distributed among a cryptocurrency's users via the internet.

Experts hold mixed opinions about investing in cryptocurrency. Because crypto is a highly speculative investment, with the potential for intense price swings, some financial advisors don't recommend people invest at all.

Bank FDs in India:

In India, 61% of total investments are Bank deposits.

Only 3% investments in Post Office and 4% in Gold.

In other words, Rs.155 lakh crores Bank Fixed deposits are there in India, which is a huge investment at very low return, because people does not trust any other asset class.

In the name of the security and assured repayment, many investors have no choice but to keep it in bank deposits, where they are getting a negative return, post inflation and taxation.

Out of all types of investments, ie Mutual funds, Real Estate, Stock Market, Term Deposits, Gold etc, the Mutual funds have delivered a better average return than any other type in the last 10 years.

But, It takes a lot of conviction and mind set, to shift to other assets from Bank deposits, because of the age old belief system.

How To Become a Billionaire in India.. for a conservative Investor who is not having the right knowledge or time to explore the stock market.

- **Invest in the market thru top wealth Managers, who manage your money.**
- **Invest in real estate, especially comml real estate in top metros.**
- **Invest in startups, like UNICORNS, where there is possibility of greater capital appreciation in shorter period.**
- **Start your own business or own service Industry, if have some family business or 2nd generation business skills and necessary zeal to start your own venture.**

Don't be a follower but become a trend setter
Make advantage of compounding
Recognize multi baggers and consistent compounders

Avoid wasteful, and unproductive expenditure and start planning at an early age, so that your financial planning is implemented without any break.

****

F

The Conclusion Estate Planning

<u>Estate planning and easy transmission of property</u>

Make your WILL as per your choice and as per your wish.

Ensure that all your loved ones aware of your assets and their details

pl. note that WILL can be prepared or modified without many legal issues.

Ensure that all your liabilities, if any, are properly insured and taken care of.

We can choose our beneficiaries and how we are going to allocate them as per our wish can be done by giving nominations and preparing a will.

Always give nominations, wherever it is available, so that the asset can be transferred to nominees, without any legal procedures and confusion.

Keep a record of all your Investments and Liabilities if any in a Proper book and preserve it safely.

Inform and discuss all your major financial decisions with your spouse, and keep a record, with photo copies and full details. Keep track of all your periodical returns and diarize it.

Don't ever mention your assets or income details with strangers or untrustworthy people.

Don't ever showcase your Gold or precious metals, or cash in public or new places.

Estate planning is one important step, in wealth management, to ensure that there is a peaceful transmission of assets to the family members and to avoid legal complications etc.

****

To Sum Up.....

To conclude:

- Firmly believe that you have the capacity and ability to compound wealth and can become a billionaire
- Follow it up with detailed plan and implement it
- Review it every quarter and if necessary, modify the strategy
- Don't ever quit your action plan, in spite of some initial setbacks
- Focus on the target, not on the other distractions
- Invest in yourself and improve your financial knowledge
- Track the performance and take advantages of emerging opportunities
- Note down the various hints and suggestions in the book and prepare your own action plan
- Maintain the company of best brains of the investors and friends
- Never settle for mediaocracy and poor quality
- Avoid negative people who discourage you

For those who could not spare their time, effort and resources, and could not wait further, pl. avail the services of Wealth Management Services, provided by the Multinational and National companies, whom you can repose trust, after due diligence, and evaluation of their performance for the last 10 years.

But the minimum amount of investment may be Rs.25 lacs to Rs.50 lacs, depending upon the terms and conditions of these companies.

Those of you who could not afford such high investment may purchase my book, where in the model templates are provided, basing on your age of your entry, risk profile, income etc. and other parameters.

It can also be prepared based on the detailed study of the various parameters, which is point based and devoid of any human emotions and sentiments. It is tailor made and customised for the each investor by the team of experts, who have been passionately doing this activity, since a decade.

You can contact for such services here....

VENKATA CHALAM RALLAPALLI
your wealth PROGRESS PARTNER
email: 085-venkata@pp.plindia.com

9 798887 722160

Printed by Libri Plureos GmbH in Hamburg,
Germany